NIMROD'S SECR[ET]
THE GREATEST CONS[PIRACY]

This conspiracy concer[ns] ...
Whatever you believe, this information will change everything.

From the Series: ***Strongholds & False Beliefs***
Doctrines of the World Order, the reign of Babel

The greatest conspiracy on Earth is officially exposed.

The Nimrod mindset is pervasive throughout all cultures in all times. All the solar deities everywhere represented the original Nimrod Sun deity in a ***babbled name***. They were all "reborn" on December 25th. Baal, Ra, Molok, Odin, Apollo, and the Gilgamesh mythology are based on Nimrod. The media will eventually come around to the fact that Santa is the modern world's Nimrod character. Mankind's most cherished religious practices are modeled after a legendary fantasy based on fertility, leaving out the knowledge of the true Creator and His redemption plan for us.

Nimrod's Secret Identity will show how mankind worships **traditions** with great zeal, and that the most cherished traditions are secretly connected to Nimrod's original rebellion, and the dragon's power.
Freemasons and other occult consortiums know this.
One Name will bring the whole World Order to its knees: **Yahusha**.
He will burn the **religion of traditions** to the ground.
None of men's traditions will survive the Second Coming.

1

Printed book ISBN: 9781495175190

By Lew White, educated by the Jesuit-Illuminati
Copyright © 2015 by Lew White
Published by Torah Institute
POB 436044, Louisville, KY 40253 USA
502-261-9833
For more information visit
fossilizedcustoms.com & torahzone.net
amazon.com
TORAH INSTITUTE'S YOUTUBE CHANNEL
Visit Facebook: Lew White, BYNV, & Torah Institute

CONTENTS

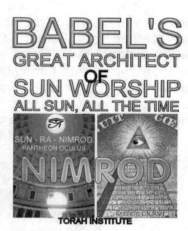

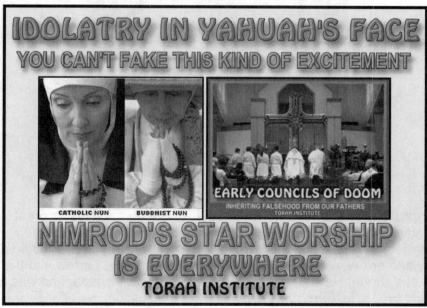

BABEL'S MOTHER OF HARLOTS:
THE REIGNING WORLD ORDER
INTRODUCTION TO NIMROD'S WORLD ORDER

Since the beginning of civilization and the first king on Earth, a struggle to control the minds (hearts) of all mankind has never ceased. It began with Nimrod, the mighty hunter of men. The worship of the host of heaven (constellations, planets, Sun, Moon, and stars) is the obvious Astrology, and also concealed in family traditions such as birthdays, Christmas, Easter, New Years Day, Mother's and Father's Days, Valentine's Day, and many other fertility celebrations. These patterns of Babel's teaching authority are intertwined with family bonds. To meddle with them causes familial bonds to break down. The World Order requires everyone to worship (serve, obey) men's traditions, not the Creator.
The World Order of Nimrod controls teachings (what we believe).
The World Order is the beast.

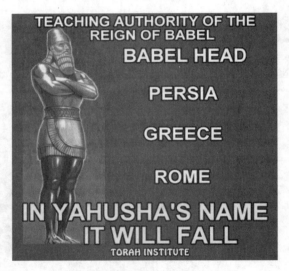

TEACHING AUTHORITY OF THE REIGN OF BABEL
BABEL HEAD
PERSIA
GREECE
ROME
IN YAHUSHA'S NAME IT WILL FALL
TORAH INSTITUTE

WHO WAS NIMROD?

Scripture tells us he was the founder of Babel, and Noak's great-grandson. A descendant of Ham (or Kam), he became a mighty hunter, of what is disputable. He is commonly portrayed as holding a bow and arrow, associated with his desire to shoot an arrow into the sky at Yahuah! He was against Yahuah, and many suspect he was a hybrid breed, a *transhuman*, possibly of the Anakim (Nephilim, meaning *fallen ones*). All the Nephilim were destroyed in the flood due to their violent and horrific behavior. They were human mutants who were extremely violent and murderous. Their genetic alterations had corrupted all flesh to the point only a few normal humans remained prior to the flood. Yahuah set His heart on destroying all living creatures that breathed air.

Noak was righteous and *"perfect in his generations"* (Gen. 6:9), so he and 7 members of his immediate family were allowed to continue the line of humanity. After the flood, the activity of the fallen malakim (angels) started up again, so the Nephilim began to reappear (Gen. 6:4, Num. 13:33). During the days of Shaul and Daud (aka king David), the champion of the Philistines, Goliath, was a giant.

The "land of Nimrod" (Micah 5:6) was later called Assyria. Genesis 10 tells us Nimrod was the first to become a "mighty one." This expression tells us he was the first human claiming to be a deity.

The historian Josephus stated Nimrod built the Tower of Babel to take revenge on Yahuah, and provide a means of escape in case Yahuah decided to flood the whole world again. After the confusion of tongues, other cultures referred to him by diverse names. Some examples of names by which he is known are: **Shamash, Utu, Orion, Osiris, Baal, Ahura Mazda, Gilgamesh, Zeus, Apollo, Surya, Woden, Krampus, Helios, Duzu, Tammuz,** etc. Many of these referred to the Sun deity in their cultures, or the offspring of the Sun deity. The Roman deity **Apollo** is the Persian deity **Mithras**. They are shown with **hunting equipment** because Nimrod was "a mighty hunter."

DID NIMROD BUILD THE TOWER OF BABEL?

Josephus (Yusef Ben MatithYahu) wrote:

"Now it was Nimrod who excited them to such an affront and contempt of Alahim. He was the grandson of Ham, the son of Noah, a bold man, and of great strength of hand. He persuaded them not to ascribe it to Alahim, as if it were through his means they were happy, *but to believe that it was their own courage which procured that happiness*. (sound familiar?) He also gradually changed the government into tyranny, seeing no other way of turning men from the fear of Alahim, but to bring them into a constant dependence on his power. He also said he would be revenged on Alahim, if he should have a mind to drown the world again; for that he would build a tower too high for the waters to reach. And that he would avenge himself on Alahim for destroying their forefathers.

Now the multitude were very ready to follow the determination of Nimrod, and to esteem it a piece of cowardice to submit to Alahim; and they built a tower, neither sparing any pains, nor being in any degree negligent about the work: and, by reason of the multitude of hands employed in it, it grew very high, sooner than anyone could expect; but the thickness of it was so great, and it was so strongly built,

5

that thereby its great height seemed, upon the view, to be less than it really was. It was built of burnt brick, cemented together with mortar, made of bitumen, that it might not be liable to admit water. When Alahim saw that they acted so madly, he did not resolve to destroy them utterly, since they were not grown wiser by the destruction of the former sinners; but he caused a tumult among them, by producing in them diverse languages, and causing that, through the multitude of those languages, they should not be able to understand one another. The place wherein they built the tower is now called Babylon, because of the confusion of that language which they readily understood before; for the Hebrews mean by the word Babel, *confusion*."

IT'S A NIMROD THING, YOU WOULDN'T UNDERSTAND

What you are reading is information that has been kept secret from the masses for millennia, held back by those in secret societies.

Their whispered secrets are being shouted from the rooftops, and their power will soon be completely removed on the Day of Yahuah.

Everything we do is patterned from behavior guided by ancient Babel's Astrology. Recognizing it, and how carefully planned and executed it is, tells us we definitely have a spiritual enemy in our midst. We've been programmed from infancy to perform rebellious activity.

When our eyes are opened to the Truth, many of us recognize how the family photos of our youth captured many events like Christmas, Easter, birthdays, Halloween, and other pagan festivities. Many of us have now ceased to observe these fertility practices, and paid a huge price for doing so. Our families and friends feel we don't love them because we no longer "walk" in our old ways: **"For we *have spent* enough of our past lifetime in doing the desire of the gentiles, having walked in indecencies, lusts, drunkenness, orgies, wild parties, and abominable idolatries, in which they are surprised that you do not run with them in the same flood of loose behavior, blaspheming, who shall give an account to Him who is ready to judge the living and the dead."** – 1 Peter 4:3-5

We know men's words will pass away, but Yahusha's Words will never pass away. The traditions everyone worships will not survive the Second Coming. It's time to wake up now.

"And whatever is concealed shall be revealed, and whatever is hidden shall be known." Luke 12:2

"I shall give you shepherds according to My heart, and they shall

feed you with knowledge and understanding." YirmeYahu / Jer. 3:15

NIMROD'S SECRET IDENTITY

All the babbled names of Nimrod (the great architect of the tower of Babel) became the "mighty ones" of the gentiles. Nimrod was worshipped as the Sun after his death, so Baal, Ahura-Mazda, Osiris, Serapis, Zeus, Apollo, and so on were only babbled names for **him**. Scripture calls the current world order the beast, which is a living animal system of **worshipping the host of heaven** (zodiac, zoo animals). The legendary Gilgamesh is also about Nimrod.
Nimrod's rebellion started all the pagan witchcraft, and the most prominent form of it is **Sun worship**, mimicked by Constantine's 4th beast model. They meet on Sunday morning, ring bells, and meet at **pillars** (steeples), just as Nimrod's ancient World Order developed it.
Nimrod built the tower of Babel to shoot an arrow into the sky, depicted by the "constellation" **Orion**. Josephus wrote that he did so in vengeance against Yahuah for sending the Great Flood. The **Nimrod secret** lies beneath all occult secrets, veiled in astrology, horoscopes, birthday celebrations, and the whole pagan calendar slowly blended into the faith in Yahusha. Yahuah repeatedly warned us to not follow the ways of the nations, yet they adopted them and dedicated them to Him (as was done with the golden calf). Pagan temples were not destroyed, they were converted into Christian houses of worship!
The **Pantheon** at Rome (built by Hadrian in 126 CE, meaning *"to all the gods"*) has been in continuous use since it was built. It is now a Catholic church, *Santa Maria ad Martyres*. If we dedicate a pagan place, object, or behavior to Yahuah, does His Word tell us to do it? Those blinded by traditions perceive Truth as "ridiculous." It disturbs them because most people want to keep on dreaming. **Tradition is religion, but Truth is reality.**

7

NIMROD - ORION - SAGITTARIUS
BABEL'S OLD RELIGION
ZODIAC - HOROSCOPE - ASTROLOGY

Fig. 14.

Bull from Nimród. From VAUX, p. 236.

PANTHEON
Rome, Italy

SANTA MARIA AD MARTYRES

THE MOST ANCIENT CONSPIRACY OF THEM ALL

"And Yahuah said to me, 'There is a *conspiracy* among the men of Yahudah and among the inhabitants of Yerushalayim. They have turned back to the crookednesses of their forefathers who refused to hear My words, and they have gone after other mighty ones to serve them. The house of Yisharal and the house of Yahudah have broken My Covenant I made with their fathers."
- YirmeYahu / Jer. 11:9-10

Instead of doing things Yahuah's way, we've inherited Babel. Our conduct either proves we serve Yahuah, or the rebel Nimrod. Nimrod became "a mighty one."

"And Kush brought forth Nimrod, he began to be a mighty one on the arets. He was a mighty hunter before Yahuah, therefore it is said, 'Like Nimrod the mighty hunter before Yahuah.'" - Gen. 10:8-9

TARGET: THE FAMILY

The family unit is the foundation of any nation. The family was created by Yahuah. In recent years it is being challenged by forces that seek to alter and corrupt Yahuah's creation. **Traditions are patterns of behavior passed from parents to their children**. A great secret kept

8

for thousands of years is being revealed by teachers of Yahuah here in the last days. Nimrod, known by many other names in many cultures of the past, exploited the strong family bonds by inserting patterns of rebellious sorcery into the family unit.

To disturb these **traditions** implanted by Nimrod is like a "kill switch" to relationships. ***Check your family photos***, and you can better detect what's been going on. Families gather together at the call of **tradition**.

CONSIDER HOW MANY OF OUR EARLY FAMILY PHOTOS
CAPTURE NIMROD'S SECRET IN THE RECORD OF OUR LIVES.
A FEW EARLY PHOTOS FROM MY OWN LIFE:

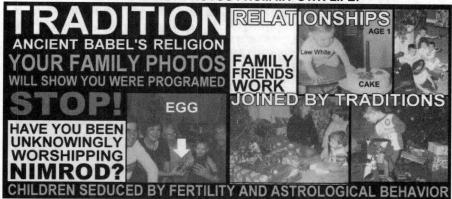

Asherah trees, wreaths, eggs, bunnies, cakes, candles - all witchcraft

The **Great Architect** of Sun worship was Nimrod, and was deified by the Babylonians. The beast's hierarchy continues to honor Nimrod as the Sun in symbolic ways using obelisks, crosses, haloes, as well as terminology and maxims.

Nimrod is the lawless antithesis of the Mashiak. Whose image and inscription is on our currency of exchange? **"IN GOD WE TRUST"** takes on a strange meaning when you look up the origin of the word GOD. Let's examine the word's origin:

WHO IS GOD?

GOD (god): **"Common Teutonic word for personal object of religious worship, FORMERLY APPLICABLE TO SUPER-HUMAN BEINGS OF HEATHEN MYTH; on conversion of Teutonic races to Christianity, TERM WAS APPLIED TO SUPREME BEING."** (Encyclopedia Americana, 1945)

Super-human beings are mentioned here. Nimrod, the mighty hunter *who became a **mighty one***, was a real man who developed into a heathen myth. This is verification that a creature is deceiving the whole world, and has successfully hood-winked the nations to conform to a pattern he instituted long ago in Babylon under **Nimrod**. Alexander Hislop (*The Two Babylons*) connected the dots (over 100 years ago) that the papacy was disguised Nimrod worship. The beast was designed and built by Nimrod, the Great Architect of the *World Order*, and the builder of the *tower of Babel*.

The **reign of Babel** will continue until Yahusha returns and takes it completely out of the way forever. Now that your eyes are opened to the Truth, you'll see the Nimrod influence everywhere.

The Freemasons secretly worship "Lucifer," the *light-bringer*.

They also revere Nimrod as the **Great Architect;** and now you know.

Nimrod has been god all along. The dragon is behind all god-worship. We don't wake up one day and do things in unison because it is the right thing to do; we're programmed with lies and futility.

SHAMMASH   WODEN   APOLLO

IT'S ALWAYS BEEN ABOUT NIMROD

If we are **not obeying**, but saying **we know Him**, we are liars, and do not know Him, **nor do we belong to Him**. (1Yn. 2:4).

The thoughts of the flesh rebel against Torah, and this is what being *"in the flesh"* means. Rom 8:7-9:

"Because the mind of the flesh is enmity towards Alahim, for it does not subject itself to the Torah of Alahim, neither indeed is it able, and those who are in the flesh are unable to please Alahim. But you are not in the flesh but in the Spirit, if indeed the Spirit of Alahim dwells in you. And if anyone does not have the Spirit of Mashiak, this one is not His."

The **reign of Babel** (the beast) programs us with traditions,
but the **reign of Yahusha** (appearing in our hearts) gives us the
perspective of the Mind of Yahuah so we do what is pleasing to Him.
We receive eyesight, and live in the Light, His Torah.
The dragon blinds, but Yahusha opens minds to His will.
Why would we be taught to do things like the pagans?
Who's running your life, Nimrod? - or Yahusha?
Those who built **high places**, **ate pigs**, and **met in the morning on
the Day of the Sun** can be found in Scripture - and the beast has
taught us to imitate *them*, and not Yahusha. Yahuah told us not to
learn the ways of the nations, or *serve Him* in their way.

UNCOVERING THE NAKEDNESS; THE BALLS (TESTICLES), TINSEL (SEMEN), AND RIBBONS (HYMEN)

PILLAR OF JEALOUSY EZ 8

ASHERAH

MAYPOLE WITH WREATH

THE ERECT POLE, HAT, TREE, OR SPIRE ARE HIDDEN SYMBOLS OF MALE FERTILITY
THE PHALLUS, AND THE ACCOMPANYING VAGINA, THE WREATH, ARE DETESTABLE

URBAN MYTHS & LEGENDS

*Some believe there are 7 sacraments that dispense grace; a tooth
fairy rewards us when we put a tooth under our pillow; and that at
some point in the future, an evil beast will arise and force
everyone to receive a tattoo on their forehead or right hand.
The weirder these myths may be, the more likely they are
believed. At the other end of the spectrum is something
called sound doctrine.*
The sound doctrine is only found in what is called the
Word, which is what Paul charged Timothy to speak (preach).

Traditions have muddled what people believe, and certainly have
replaced the Word, because the Word Paul referred to is the
TORAH --- this is the "Word" which Yahuah constantly refers to
that He wishes all men to repent to, and OBEY.
Without having been programmed by the TORAH, the message or
report we often hear goes into our ears and cannot be heard and
understood. The TORAH is the Covenant that Yahuah made with
Yisharal, the only people on Earth He has His Covenant with.
Foreigners must ENGRAFT into the commonwealth of Yisharal
through the Covenant in order to take part in the promises
Yahuah has made to His people (Romans 11).

11

False teachers tell us that to live according to TORAH is evil, and proclaim it to be "legalism" . . . as if being legal is far from Yahuah's will for us. Can obedience be abhorrent to Yahuah? Yahusha walked according to the Torah, otherwise He would sin. It will be illegalism that will cause the vast majority of people to be caste into the lake of fire.

Paul told Timothy all about the MYTHS people would turn aside to, shunning the sound doctrine at 2 Tim 4:1-5:

"In the presence of Alahim and of Mashiak Yahusha, Who will judge the living and the dead, and in view of His appearing and His Reign, I give you this charge:

Preach the Word; be prepared in season and out of season; correct, rebuke and encourage-with great patience and careful instruction. For the time will come when men will not put up with sound doctrine. Instead, to suit their own desires, they will gather around them a great number of teachers to say what their itching ears want to hear. They will turn their ears away from the truth and turn aside to myths.

But you, keep your head in all situations, endure hardship, do the work of an evangelist, discharge all the duties of your ministry."

CAN THE POPE FORGIVE SIN?

Let's reason together about that. Sin is a debt. If a *man* offends another *man*, the offending man has incurred a **debt**.

To discharge that debt (forgive the debt), the offended person is the only one who may retain or remove it.

The reason only Yahuah is able to remove (discharge) an offense against Him is because He established the wisdom of Torah, not men. Men cannot legitimately make their own Torah, but if they do, they feed on "wormwood." This is what we are witnessing here. If a mere man has offended another mere man, a mere man may forgive or retain the debt. We ask Yahuah to forgive us our debts "as" we forgive others their debts.

If we think we can forgive someone's offenses in place of Yahuah, we blaspheme the Name and Throne of the universe. The "Nimrod mindset" resides among us as a teaching authority, but those who have received the Spirit of Yahusha are given discernment to follow only Him. He calls us His branches. He is the Root, and we are branches of His teachings. This means the pope is in great error, and he has no authority to forgive a woman for murdering her unborn child - but Yahusha does. **The pope can't forgive his own sins, or anyone else's.** If someone threw a pie in his face, the most he can do is forgive the one that threw it. Men's authoritarian religions are all modeled after Babel's original blueprint.

In Nimrod's Magisterium, the kingpin that represents the power of Nimrod is like a deity, and even *claims to be one*. If given the chance, they would eliminate all other citadels of power. When its power was at its height, the world was the darkest (hence, the *Dark Ages*). If that power was restored to it, it would be like living in a Hobbit story all the time, and mankind would be even more enslaved than it already is. In the fantasy world of religion, the Mother Circe (church) claims the authority to be in the place of Yahuah on Earth, and able to forgive sins.

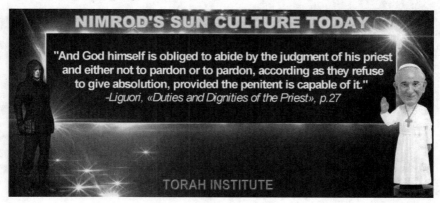

NIMROD'S SUN CULTURE TODAY

"And God himself is obliged to abide by the judgment of his priest and either not to pardon or to pardon, according as they refuse to give absolution, provided the penitent is capable of it."
-Liguori, «Duties and Dignities of the Priest», p.27

TORAH INSTITUTE

VICAR OF NIMROD

The papacy claims to be the "vicar" (one in place of) Yahusha. In reality, he is the vicar of Nimrod.

The priest (one who has received the psuedo-sacrament of "holy orders") pretends to be endowed with powers to dispense "absolution" for sins committed by a penitent. Usually they submit a "penance" that involves necromancy, such as praying to the dead using a device called a rosary. This item comes from Hinduism, along with the "holy water" (connected with the Ganges river) as so many other practices do. The Nimrod mindset is all about tradition, and the imaginary "apostolic succession" they offer as the source of their authority. Yahusha's Natsarim receive authority to teach from Him, not a human ordination. When Yahusha infuses His presence into one of His followers, Yahusha Himself walks in power through them. Human institutions are not reality, they are religion. They pretend to operate their spells just as the actors on the Starship Enterprise pretend the cardboard props are operational systems.

After Babel, cultures used the Nimrod model of Sun worship. Nimrod, Semiramis, and Tammuz are the source of the Trinitarian format. The names were babbled because Yahuah had confused the languages. When we investigate the similarities of all pagan customs, they all follow the original very closely. All Sun deities share a common "birthday." December 25th – and winter solstice of the ancient world –

was the time the Sun was "reborn." We quickly catch-on to the trend, and realize that Zeus is Nimrod; Gilgamesh is Nimrod; Molok is Nimrod; Osiris is Nimrod; Serapis is Nimrod; Helios is Nimrod; Ahura Mazda is Nimrod; and the list goes on. They're all Nimrod.

Even **Santa is Nimrod.**

NIMROD WAS DEIFIED AS THE SUN

ALL SUN DEITIES ARE BABBLED FORMS OF NIMROD'S NAME

ALL SUN DEITIES' BIRTHDAYS WERE CELEBRATED ON DECEMBER 25

NIMROD IS SANTA TORAH INSTITUTE

NIMROD TRINITIES EXPRESSED IN PERSIAN, CELTIC, HINDU, AND EGYPTIAN CULTURES

TRINITARIAN ORIGIN: BABEL

The triangle and triquetra in all religious imagery represents *creation, preservation, and destruction*. Babel's Trinity, Nimrod, Semiramis, and Tammuz are reflected in Hinduism's Brahma, Vishnu, and Shiva. Amun, Re, and Ptah became the Egyptian triad. Sumeria's astrology imprinted every culture with the worship of the host of heaven, trinities, fertility symbols, human sacrifices, reincarnation, and the concept of ascending into the heavens to live among the deities after death.

REINCARNATION ORIGIN

The cycle of "rebirth" (reincarnation) originates from Babel's trinity, Nimrod, Semiramis, and Tammuz. After Nimrod was slain and ascended to the heavens to become the Sun, Semiramis was found to carry his child by having been impregnated by the rays of the Sun. Tammuz was born as Nimrod reincarnated.

14

NIMROD THE HERO IN NORSE MYTHOLOGY

Nimrod was characterized as the Sun deity Woden (Odin) by Norse tribes. The name Odin is derived from the Hebrew word ADON, which was ATON in Egypt. It means *sovereign*. The Viking triquetra symbol represents the Norse Trinity, Woden, Frigga (Frey), and Thor. This and many other Trinitarian symbols were adopted by Christianity. Babel's trinity is babbled widely even among the same population. Thor is "Teutates" reborn as Taranis, yet in each case Nimrod's character is expressed. The classical writer Lucan (2nd century CE) refers to Teutates as a member of the Celtic trinity, along with Esus and Taranis.

ODIN RIDING SLEIPNIR   **TRIQUETRA**

WHAT THE WHO? WEEKDAYS GET THEIR NAMES FROM PAGAN IDOLS?

WHAT?

TORAH INSTITUTE

NIMROD'S SECRET IDENTITY

Woden, Thor, Frey, and Teutates give the names to four of the profane days of the week:

Tuesday (Tiu's Day) Mardi = Day-of-Mars (if you speak French, think MARdi = MARS-di), Mars is the Roman god of war. The Roman calendar is also Pagan, and this deity names the third month, March. The Teutonic / Celtic folk called this day "Tiu Daeg." Tiu was the imaginary son of Woden and Frigga, imaginary Celtic (Druid) idols.

Wednesday (Wodin's Day), ODIN or Woden, the chief deity of the Norse, who commanded the Valkries and rode an eight-legged steed called Sleipnir, a horse born to LOKI. Woden was believed to be the husband of Frigga, and father of Thor. Woden was imagined to ride his 8-legged horse (Sleipnir) in Valhalla, the Celtic idea of heaven. The eight legs seem to be reflected in the 8-reindeer of the jolly old elf, aka *Krampus*, or Santa Claus (*"Saint Ni-cholas"*). Nimrod is hiding in plain sight as a Sun deity hero of children, the same character as **Molok**, the abomination of the Moabites:

Thursday (Thor's Day) The Norse deity of thunder and son of Woden, also known as Taranus, or the Dutch Donner (a name bestowed on one of Santa's reindeer). Corresponding to the Romans' day of Jupiter (in French, "JEUdi" is pretty close to "Jove-day." Jove is another name for the Roman god Jupiter -- as in the exclamation, "By Jove!").
Friday (Freya's Day) Also known as Frigga, the wife of Woden, her *emblem was the fish* (fertility again). The young fish are called "fry," from her name. Catholics could tell you about how and when a fish-fry occurs, but they adopted it from the Pagans. The Romans called her Astarte, or Venus.
By whatever name, she is the Earth Mother, Semiramis (Babel's Mother of Harlots, aka Ishtar/Easter), Asherah, Astaroth, Gaia, Durga, Nanna, and so on. The Greeks honored Aphrodite on this day.
Esus (or Hesus) is another Norse Hero (Nimrod figure). Human victims were sacrificed to Esus by being tied to a tree and flailed (skinned alive).

THE MAGISTERIUM

The great Mystery Babylon has always been here, and exists to control what the world believes. The Latin word **"magisterium"** means *teaching authority,* and the Greek word is **"didascalia."** The church fathers of Christianity were seated at Alexandria, Egypt, and referred to themselves as the *Didascalia.* The Roman Catholic seat of power at

Rome calls itself the Magisterium. Nimrod's original control over humanity was empowered by the dragon. The centralization of power gave the dragon the ability to control what everyone believes. That power and authority never lost its continuity, and it resides in the **totalitarian magisterium** the world calls the Roman Catholic Church. It has always been here since the founding of Babel, but has gone by many other names. The most recent form of this beastly world government grew from Roman roots, which openly worshipped the Sun deity Apollo Sol Invictus. This is the 4th beast, blended with all the sorcery and witchcraft of the former 3 beasts. Constantine merged, or synthesized, diverse Sun worshipping bodies together into a universal pattern of behavior. Mithraism, Zoroastrianism, Hinduism, and Manichaen customs were blended into a new mold, and these pagan forms of witchcraft came together into a new shape.

There is a Baby in this dirty bathwater, and when we remove Him from all the surrounding filth, you will recognize how the whole world has been deceived.

This beastly World Order channels Babel's power in three divisions: Clergy-Nobility-Laity. It has been so since the days of Nimrod, the Great Architect of the World Order. This magisterium is Babel going under another name, and all the reigns of the Earth are controlled as surely as a beast is controlled by a ring in its nose. Babel's world government poses as a religious institution. Over the centuries it has set up a list of "dogmas" and requires its adherents to accept them with absolute devotion. This beast behaves like a chameleon, adopting the practices and symbols of indigenous populations and changing their meaning. Behind all the symbols and practices is the ancient religion of Babel: Sun worship, and the worship of the "host of heaven."

This organization considers itself the only path to salvation through its dogmas. Salvation is understood to be solely through the dispensation of seven sacraments, available exclusively through the priesthood of the "one true mother church." Failure to believe in any one dogma is grounds for excommunication. For many centuries those who resisted the authority of this mother church were burned at the stake as heretics.

This magisterium is the source of such doctrines as **Purgatory, eternal suffering in fire, relic kissing (veneration of human remains), transubstantiation (bread wafer transforms into living body and blood of Yahusha with words "hoc est corpus meum"), statue veneration (kneeling before objects), steeples/sun pillars, bells, worship of the "host" (in a monstrance – sun burst object), prayers to the dead (necromancy via rosaries), monks, nuns, popes, priests, celibacy, indulgences, trinity doctrine, infant** baptism, apostolic succession, sacraments, crosses (symbol of Sun deity everywhere throughout history), replacement of Name Yahuah to "LORD" (Baal), adoption of Easter / Ishtar fertility festival with sunrise worship & egg/bunny/fish symbols, Natalis Sol Invictus (Saturnalia) transformed into "Christ-Mass," a celebration of Yahusha's birth, - and much more.

They are generally doing everything Yahuah ordered not to be done, while ignoring everything He told us to guard and observe. They forbade the Scriptures from the "laity" (laity means "the people," the bottom level of their **World Order** of clergy-nobility-laity, or *3 estates*).

This magisterium is the source from which Protestants have inherited many of their doctrines and behavior. The belief in *"one god in three persons"* **defines** Catholicism according to Athanasius, one of the attendees of the Nicene Council in 325. Athanasius was from Alexandria's Didascalia (teaching authority), and is dubbed the *"father of orthodoxy." Ortho-doxy* literally means *"upright teaching."* **Natsarim** throughout history were considered heretics by this teaching authority, and were held to be *anathema* (worthy of death).

Natsarim work to teach the Truth, and reject the teaching authority of the magisterium, and all those following its rebellious practices. Everything in the list above is witchcraft, carefully fed to the masses over many centuries. Abiding in Yahuah's Word sets us free from false beliefs.

"So Yahusha said to those Yahudim who believed Him,
'If you stay in My Word, you are truly My taught ones, and you shall know the truth, and the truth shall make you free.'" Yn. 8:31-32

The belief that Yahuah, Who wrote the Torah, sent His Son to abolish the Torah, is illogical.

The changing of the Torah by Constantine (prophesied at Dan. 7:25) does not change it, it is **an attempt** to change it. The 7th day of the week was blessed, and set-apart by Yahuah, so we see in the Millennial reign "from Shabath to Shabath" all flesh will bow to Him. This will not be the Day of the Sun each week. Yahusha told us in the last days to "pray your flight will not be in winter,or on the Shabath."

Heaven and Earth are still here, and until these both pass away, we must stand only on the foundation laid by Yahusha, since we are to **"walk even as He walked."** Constantine said, "let us have nothing in common with the hostile rabble of the Yahudim."

Since it seems the Natsarim "live in Old Testament times" in contrast to those who follow Constantine and the circus fathers' allegorical interpretations, how can we dismiss Is. 8:20, and this clear statement from 1 Yn. 2:4-7:

"The one who says, 'I know Him,' and does not guard His commands, is a liar, and the truth is not in him. But whoever guards His Word, truly the love of Alahim has been perfected in him. By this we know that we are in Him. The one who says he stays in Him ought himself also to walk, even as He walked. Beloved, I write no fresh command to you, but an old command which you have had from the beginning. The old command is the Word which you heard from the beginning."

The "old Command is the **Word** which you heard from the beginning" were altered in 321 CE by Constantine and his "**Sun-day**."

WERE YOU TAUGHT THERE ARE SACRAMENTS?

When the Star Trek crew pretends the cardboard fixtures they fiddle with are real, operational weapons, tractor beams, or transporters, those watching also pretend they are real. It's a fantasy, but while it is happening everyone pretends it is real. Religion is the same imaginary pretense. Reality is where we need to be, so we will become sober. We need de-programming. In Latin, the words *hoc es corpus meum* literally mean "this is My body." These words spoken originally in Hebrew by Yahusha *were pointing to Himself, and His body of followers.* We are His body, and He is the Head of His body.

19

The "unleavened" aspect represented that body (1 Cor 5:7), uncorrupted by the teachings of men. The *teachings of men* are referred to in Scripture as *leaven*.

He is the Head; and we His body partake of His sufferings. Instead of Passover, the Circus calls the repeated ritual of remembering Yahusha's death *"the sacrifice of the Mass"* and a *"bloodless sacrifice."* In this ritual, it was believed the common bread **transubstantiates** into the *living body* of Yahusha. This concept caused even more idolatry, such as genuflecting to the *"Host."* It encourages literal worship and prayer to a displayed "Host" in an object called a monstrance. *This violates the first, second, and third Commandments.*

These teachings are abominations in the cup of Circe (a name for the woman, aka Babel), causing the world to become drunken (mad), and such idolatry keeps the world unclean before the Throne of Yahuah, incurring His blazing wrath on the Day of Yahuah:

"Flee from the midst of Babel, and let each one save his life! Do not be cut off in her crookedness, for this is the time of the vengeance of Yahuah, the recompense He is repaying her. Babel was a golden cup in the hand of Yahuah, making drunk all the Earth. The nations drank her wine, that is why the nations went mad!" - Jer / YirmeYahu 51:6, 7 (see also 2 Pet 3, ZekarYah 14, Malaki 4, 1 Thess 5,2 Thess 1, Mt 24, Yual [Joel] 2)

Worship of the Host in a sunburst monstrance is idolatry.

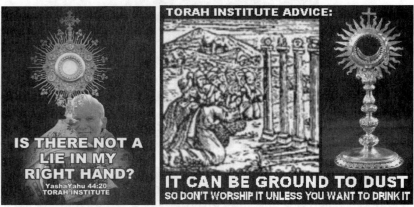

The worship of the "host of heaven" (Acts 7:42) involved the zodiac; the sun, moon, and stars, and one of the elements was the image of the crux, which depicted the *equinoxes* (the intersection of the celestial meridian and the celestial equator twice each year).

THE WITNESS OF YAHUSHA (GREAT COMMISSION)

There is a distinction between the true witness of Yahusha, and the false one. Just before He departed, Yahusha instructed us to teach the Name and obedience to His Commandments to all nations.

Constantine's Christianity does not hold to the witness of Yahusha; the behavior and symbols reflect Rome's indigenous practices of Sun worship. It avoids anything to do with the culture of Yisharal (Israel), especially the Torah of Yahuah.

Another way of saying witness or testimony is "great commission." The false witness denies His Name, and expects everyone to tithe to its teaching authority while not teaching His Commandments (Torah, love-training).

I'm sure as Natsarim we can all agree our mission is to be ready at every opportunity to share the Name and the Word with all who will listen, and not worry about selecting which kind of soil they may be - that's Yahusha's business with those who hear us.

The mission has never changed since the giving of the Torah at Sinai, but this time we are empowered by Yahusha's Spirit to understand its goal of love. The same mission to the nations was given to Yisharal, but only "given;" it had not been "received" until Yahusha entered the hearts of His people, the first Natsarim.

If we look foolish to those in the world, so-be-it; we're the counter-culture choosing to live in peace with all men by becoming servants rather than overlords. Constantine's Christianity is not the testimony of Yahusha, it's Babel's great commission of "believe and be lawless." Natsarim are to spread the word of restoration to favor.

Our highest purpose for being here is not sitting in a pew believing something. We are to be used as vessels to plead that the lost be restored to favor by obeying Yahusha's orders for us.

What were we told to do?

We were commissioned as envoys to all men everywhere:

There's a Hebrew idiom, ***"going out and coming in."*** It has to do with our interaction with the outside world and how engaged we are with it. It's only by Yahusha's power we can do anything, and it may be premature to say His witness is unable to take different approaches.

AN ANECDOTE

Not long ago, two Jehovah's Witnesses came to my door, but they did not have the witness of Yahusha, only their *Jesus*, and *their form* of Constantine's Christianity.

When I told them the Name was **Yahusha**, and it meant ***"I am your Deliverer,"*** they said ***"Jesus is His Name in English."***

So I asked them what "Jesus" meant in English. Silence followed.

Next I tested them on the Word by asking them, ***"Which day is the Sabbath day?"*** Silence again. Then one of them said, ***"We came out to talk to you, not to listen to what _you_ have to say."***

Obviously, the witness of Yahusha is not well known, but we should take every opportunity we find ourselves in to allow **Him to speak through us.** Without Him, we can do nothing.

Although I can see no harm in going out into the world and doing exactly what they were doing, it would be more effective if they did so with the Truth. It certainly would not be wrong in Yahusha's eyes at all. We are not all used in the same way, and I would never want to disparage the work given to another follower of Yahusha. In my case, He had me sitting there waiting to answer the door; but He spoke His witness into their ears, and seed was planted.

WE ARE RESTORED BY YAHUSHA'S BLOOD ATONEMENT

"And all *matters* are from Alahim, who has restored us to favor with Himself through Yahusha Mashiak, and has given us the service of restoration to favor, that is, that Alahim was in Mashiak restoring the world to favor to Himself, not reckoning their trespasses to them, and has committed to us the word of restoration to favor.

Therefore we are envoys on behalf of Mashiak, as though Alahim were pleading through us. We beg, on behalf of Mashiak:

Be restored to favour with Alahim." -2Cor 5:18-20

Yahusha gave His highest orders to **His Natsarim as He left them. These orders are what we call the Great Commission**, and involve the two highest subjects of all; His **Name** and His **Word** (Ps 138:2).

"And Yahusha came up and spoke to them, saying,

'**All authority has been given to Me in shamayim and on arets. Therefore, go** (make haste, run) **and make taught ones of all the nations, immersing them in the Name of the Father and of the Son and of the Set-apart Spirit, teaching them to guard all that I have commanded you. And see, I am with you always, until the end of the age.'" Amin** (truly). —Mt 28:18-20

As time passed, the original meaning of those orders became watered-down by traditions. We are not seeing "everything" He commanded them being taught, because Constantine made sure Christians would have *"nothing in common with the hostile rabble of the Yahudim."* Yahusha intended the nations to be taught to guard *"every Word that proceeds from the mouth of Yahuah"* in order to live.

Does the context at Mt. 28 imply that this message was only for His Natsarim of that time, or did Yahusha intend for all of us to be found doing what He said when He comes? After giving the orders Yahusha said, **"And see, I am with you always, until the end of the age."** v 20

If the orders He gave were only for the Natsarim He was *speaking with,* and not to be continued to be taught to all nations throughout the time He is away, many parables would lose their meaning for us, such as the parable of the *mina*, the *sowing of the seed*, and others.

If Yahusha was intending the orders to be only for those first followers and not us, then His comment **"I am with you always"** was also only for those first followers.

But context will not allow this interpretation, since *He is with us*, and will be to the **"end of the age."**

KEFA (Peter) **ASKS IF IT WAS FOR THEM, OR ALL:**

"And Kefa said to Him, 'Master, do You speak this parable to us, or also to all?' And the Master said, 'Who then is the trustworthy and wise manager, whom his master shall appoint over his household, to give the portion of food in due season? Blessed is that servant whom his master shall find so doing when he comes.'" – Luke 12:41-43

Yahusha's followers are to perform His orders to "the end of the age." Teaching the **Name** and the **Word** is our purpose for being Natsarim in the end of days.

The highest pursuit of all is to learn how to love, and be loved.

The Great Commission is to teach the instructions of love to all, but it has been interpreted as being religious instead. If one reads the instructions as being our best hope in learning how to love, it will dispel the false idea of being about religion. The universe obviously didn't create itself.

The One that created the universe expressed the highest possible thoughts of love, and how to live that love, in His Ten Commandments.

REPAIRERS OF THE BREACH

The Ten Commandments are the "eternal" Covenant, and they teach us how to love Yahuah, and love our neighbor - they are not difficult, they are our great commission to teach, the "old paths" in which to dwell. Natsarim are the repairers of the breach before the reapers come on the Day of Yahuah. The 7th day of each week is also called **"the set-apart Day of Yahuah."**

Isa / YashaYahu 58:12-14:

"And those from among you shall build the old waste places. You shall raise up the foundations of many generations. And you would be called the Repairer of the Breach, the Restorer of Streets to Dwell In.

If you do turn back your foot from the Shabath, from doing your pleasure on My set-apart day, and shall call the Shabath 'a delight,' the set-apart day of Yahuah 'esteemed,' and shall esteem it, not doing your own ways, nor finding your own

pleasure, nor speaking your own words, then you shall delight yourself in Yahuah. And I shall cause you to ride on the heights of the earth, and feed you with the inheritance of YaAqob your father. For the mouth of Yahuah has spoken!"

Paul's writings are misunderstood by the lawless, as Peter explained. Paul explains at Colossians 2 how the **"shadows of things to come for the body of Yahusha"** outline our **redemption**. Yahusha has sealed us with His Name for the **day of our redemption**, which is one of those shadows: **Yom Kafar**, when reapers are unleashed to harvest the Earth (see book, REAPERS). Most will be burned, but the first-fruits will be protected by the same seraphim doing the reaping. The weeds are removed first, then the wheat is gathered into the New Yerushalayim.

The redemptive shadows were rejected by Constantine, since the whole culture of Torah was abhorred by his direct order. The interpretation of Paul by the lawless circus fathers was revealed by Paul himself at Acts 20 when he spoke with the elder Natsarim of his own time. He said men would arise from them who were savage wolves, not sparing the flock. When the Light dawns on you, you will see Psalm 1 and Psalm 119 as being the pure thoughts of Yahuah's plan for all mankind. (see also Eccl. 12:13, Rev. 12, Rev. 14). Anyone who annuls the least of the Commandments will be the least in the reign of Yahusha, but he who guards and teaches them will be the greatest.

LEGALISM or ILLEGALISM?

Being "legal" is thought of as heretical to today's religious leadership. The term *legalist* is a way of shaming anyone attempting to obey the will of Yahuah as it is written, and walk as Yahusha walked.
The term legalist is used as a synonym for *heretic*.
Obedience proves our faith, and when our faith is perfected in such a way that we are being "legal" in Yahuah's eyes, He knows by our active obedience that we love Him. One cannot prove their commitment to Yahuah by being illegal, and having no plan to become legal, and show improvement in that direction. 2 Peter 1 advises us to increase in our uprightness, and thereby do our utmost in making firm our calling.
The Pharisees were fakers, and obeyed the traditions of men rather than seek to obey Yahuah from their hearts.
Yahusha was never upset at them for being legal and **obeying Torah**, but rather for substituting the **traditions of men** in place of obeying Yahuah - *exactly where we find ourselves today with the illegalists in Christian leadership.*
Church tradition, not Torah, is their focus.

They want our tithe, but they don't teach the righteousness of Yahuah, His Ten Commandments.

We are ambassadors of the coming reign of Yahusha, and very much seek to be the greatest legalists of all as we purify our walk and wait for the coming of our Master. We're ironing the wrinkles out of our wedding garments, and trimming our lamps with the extra oil He is pouring into our hearts - the wisdom of the five wise virgins is knowing what is pleasing to Him.

We beg, be restored to favor with Yahuah; He is coming sooner than you expect.

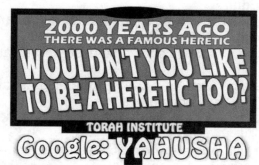

ORIGIN OF THE WORD CHRISTIAN

XPISTIANOS Found 3 times in the Received Text (NT)

The term *Christian* was used by the Greek culture several hundred years before Yahusha's birth in Bethlehem.

Rome (Italy) and Alexandria (Egypt) were the western world's primary repositories of knowledge.

A merger of ancient Egyptian, Greek, and Roman cultures took place from 300 BCE to 200 CE, and Christianity emerged from it.

The Greek deity **Serapis** replaced Osiris as the consort of Isis, and the devotees of this deity were called "**Christians**."

Hadrian (Roman emperor 117 to 138) built the **Pantheon** (temple to all gods) using concrete to form the world's largest domed structure (domes are a pagan design).

He wrote that **Serapis** and **IESU** were the *same deity*.

This is syncretism, and when it catches on, it becomes tradition. **People serve traditions with ferocious zeal.**

Confusion and syncretism between pagan cultures at Rome and Alexandria continued into the 4th century CE.

The Alexandrian cult, or *church fathers*, worked feverishly to synthesize paganism with the Messianic movement, hatching their brand under the Serapis' followers' name, *Christians*, who occupied the city for centuries before them.

The followers of Yahusha were called **Natsarim** (branches, watchmen, guardians – see Acts 24:5). We guard (shamar) the Name and the

Word. To the Greeks, the impaled Mashiak is foolishness (1 Cor. 1:23), so the Greek term "**xpristianos**" (meaning *idiot*) seemed appropriate to them.

The Greek term CHRISTIANOS in that day was a term foisted on them, causing suffering as Peter writes about it at 1 Peter 4:15-16.

No one would ever want to be labeled a murderer, thief, doer of evil, or meddler. Nor would they wish to be known as an idiot or *"cretin."*

Look at the **context** of this rarely-used term, **christianos**:

"For do not let any of you suffer as a murderer, or thief, or doer of evil, or as a meddler.

But if (*one suffers*) **as a xpistianos, let him not be ashamed, but let him esteem Alahim in this matter."** – 1 Peter 4:15-16

Some say the word xpistianos should be used only as an adjective: "*Christian* faith."

But in truth, it became used as a pronoun to denigrate and shame the Natsarim. It was a term of contempt and scorn.

If you look up the origin of the word **cretin**, you'll see the Greek source is xpistianos.

We should never **call one another** such a term. It means *an idiot,* but revisionism has caused mass-amnesia.

Please Google the term CRETIN, and learn the truth.

I ASKED THE MAGISTERIUM A QUESTION

The following question was asked from the AskACatholic web site on Saturday, August 15, 2015 at 02:59 PM, Lew White wrote:

"Yahusha's teaching authority was questioned by the chief priests and elders at Mt. 21:23. They, like the existing Magisterium, had set up their own authority, above Scripture.

What is the name of the one you worship?

And, if you claim it is Yahuah, what example of obedience to Him can you offer as a sign of that worship?

As Christianity evolved over many centuries, many alterations occurred such that resting from work on the Sabbath became **transferred** to the first day, and abstaining from unclean animals was no longer required. As there are no examples given from Scripture of these and many other practices now adopted, it has been said that "Church tradition" retains authority to do the very same things that enraged Yahusha's wrath about the Sanhedrin in His day. In this context, praying to dead people (necromancy and divination) would seem to be another example of such church tradition.

If Yahuah does not change, and such things are an abomination to Him, by what authority do you do these things, and by what name do you call on for deliverance?" - Lew White

AskACatholic responded by sharing links to pages with prepared answers. One mentioned how the Catholics wrote the Bible, for Catholics, for use in the Church. My simple questions went unanswered, and I still didn't know who they claim to worship.

My reply to them follows:
The Roman Catholic dogmas don't reveal who is being worshipped. Clearly, if I obey the 4th Commandment to rest on the 7th day, I'm a heretic (according to the Council of Laodicea, 365 CE). Catholics did not write or give us Scripture.

The first followers of Yahusha were not Catholics. Yahusha is not a Catholic. The assembly is not an institution, but a body controlled by Yahusha, the Head. The dogmas of Catholicism reveal a very different pattern of behavior than Yahusha's walk:

ROMAN CHURCH TIMELINE OF DOGMAS
(from the Catholic Encyclopedia)

DATE / DOGMA
CE 300 Full immersion changed to affusion (sprinkle).
CE 300 Prayers to the dead. NECROMANCY, a form of divination (Against Dt. 18:11 & YashaYahu 8:19)
CE 310 Making the "sign" of the CROSS.
CE 325 Anathema (death) decreed to anyone who adds or changes the creed of faith of Nice. (See years 1545 & 1560). EASTER was established at Nicea.
CE 365-370 Council of Laodicea rejects Apocrypha, calls Shabath observers "Judaizers", worthy of death. This council refers to "Shabath" as distinct from the *LORD's Day* (Baal's Day).
CE 375 Veneration of angels and dead saints (Veneration means worship)
CE 394 Institution of the **Sacrament of the Mass**:
Missa Recitata, Low Mass, priest + 1
Missa Cantata, Sung Mass, priest + 1
Missa Solemnis, High Mass, priest + 2
Missa Pontificalis, Bishop + priest + ?
CE 431 The worship of Miryam (Mary) [veneration is worship]
CE 431 Miryam "Queen of Heaven" (against YirmeYahu 7:18, 44:17, 44:25)
CE 431 Miryam "ever virgin" (against Mt. 1:25, Mk. 6:3, Yn. 2:2-4).
CE 431 Miryam "Mediatrix" (against 1 Tim. 2:5, Yn. 11:28).
CE 500 Priestcraft began to dress in "priestly garb".
CE 526 Sacrament of "Extreme Unction"
CE 593 Doctrine of "Purgatory" (against Yn. 5:24, 1Yn. 1:7-9, 2:1,2, Romans 8:1)
CE 600 Latin language only language permitted for prayer (against 1 Cor. 14:9)

CE 709 Kissing the feet of pope is ordered (against Acts 10:25,26, Rev. 19:10, 22:8,9)

CE 750 Temporal Power of pope declared (against Mt. 4:8,9, 20:25,26, Yn. 18:38)

CE 754 Council of Constantinople ordered removal of all images and abolition of image worship.

CE 785 Miryam "co-redemptrix" (against Acts 4:12, Ps. 146:5, Hebrews 7:25)

CE 788 Miryam "worship" (against Romans 1:25, Yasha Yahu 42:8, Mk. 3:21)

CE 788 Worship of cross, relics, and images re-authorized (against Ex. 20:4, Dt. 12:3, 27:15, Ps. 115:4-8)

CE 850 Fabrication and use of "holy water" (adopted from Hinduism's sacred water of the Ganges River)

CE 890 Veneration of St. Yosef, husband of Miryam. (see CE 788 listings)

CE 965 Baptism of the bells ~ ceremony of "baptizing" bells to ward off demons and to call the elect to vespers when blessed bells are rung.

CE 995 Canonization of dead saints (against Romans 1:7, 1 Cor. 1:2)

CE 998 Fasting on "Fri-days" & during "Lent" (against Mt. 15:11, 1 Cor. 10:25, 1 Tim. 4:1-8)

CE 1079 Celibacy of priestcraft declared (married priests ordered to cast-off wives, against 1 Tim. 3:2-5, 3:12, Mt. 8:14,15).

CE 1090 Institution of rosary prayer beads, or *chaplet* (against Mt. 6:7, Dt. 18:10,11 YashaYahu 8:19 ~ also, Buddhism, Shinto, and Islam practice prayer-bead counting)

CE 1190 Sale of indulgences (against Eph. 2:8-10). For those of you who don't know, this was a practice of people paying the clergy to have punishment time taken off from burning in "Purgatory" after their death. Eating meat on Friday is a "mortal" sin, so you can't buy an indulgence for doing that – it's straight to hell for you.

CE 1215 Dogma of Transubstantiation declared (against Luke 22:19,20, Mk. 13:21, Yn. 6:35, Mt. 24:23-28, 1 Cor. 11:26)

Many were burned at the stake over this false teaching.

CE 1215 Confession of sins to priest ordered (against Ps. 51:1-10, Luke 7:48 & 15:21, 1 Yn. 1:8,9)

CE 1220 Adoration of the wafer host (matsah worship! Against Ex. 20:4, Yn. 4:24)

CE 1229 Scriptures forbidden to laymen (against Yn. 5:39, 8:31, 2 Tim. 3:15-17)

CE 1265 Miryam's house moved by angel to Lorento Italy. (as fishy as this smells, I don't think they violated Torah, unless they were lying ~ what do you think?)

CE 1287 Scapular protection decreed (brown cloth talisman with picture of virgin packed with tea leaves proclaimed to contain supernatural powers or "virtues" to protect wearer

CE 1414 "Chalice" forbidden to laity at "communion" (a radical distortion of the Passover Seder, the annual remembrance of Yahusha's death)

CE 1439 Dogma of seven sacraments (against Mt. 28:19,20, & 26:26-28)

CE 1439 Purgatory declared valid dogma (against Mt. 25:46, Luke 23:43)

CE 1508 Miryam "Mother of GOD" (against Mt. 12:46-50, Lk. 8:19-21, Acts 1:14)

CE 1545 Church tradition equal and able to alter Scripture (against Mt. 15:6, Mk. 7:7-13, Col. 2:8 ~ also adds many other dogma to Council of Nice)

CE 1560 Creed of pope Pius IV decreed (against Gal. 1:8)

CE 1580 Pope declared to be *LORD GOD* (that's enough to get some people roasted. Yahuah will not allow His esteem to go to another YashaYahu 48:11)

CE 1593 *Ave Maria* adopted (means *hail Miryam*)

CE 1710 Stuffed donkey in Verona, Italy, at Church of the Madonna of the Organs, decreed to be the actual animal Yahusha ha Mashiak entered Yerushaliyim on. Visiting it will gain indulgences. Circus animals for the circus!

[When I first heard about this, I couldn't stop laughing for 10 minutes]

CE 1854 Immaculate Conception of Virgin Miryam (against Romans 3:23, & 5:12, Ps. 51:5, YirmeYahu 17:9)

CE 1864 Miryam "sinless" (against Luke 1:46, 47, Romans 3:10-19, & 23).

CE 1870 Papal infallability decreed (against 2 Thess. 2:2-12, Rev. 17:1-9, 13:5-8, 18)

CE 1907 All sciences condemned. (Science is the search for Truth, and the word comes from the Latin word, scio, *to know*)

CE 1922 Pope declared to be "Jesus Christ"

CE 1930 All public schools condemned.

CE 1950 Declaration of the bodily assumption of the Virgin Miryam into Heaven

CE 2008 The Name "Yahweh" forbidden in liturgy, singing, or worship.

CE 2014 Following Pope Francis on Twitter gains indulgences.

Here is the next reply from AskACatholic's website:

"Catholic or Roman Catholics worship Jesus Christ and ONLY Jesus Christ. Jesus founded ONE Church on St. Peter (Matthew 16:17-19) and said the gates of Hell would not prevail against the Church HE FOUNDED on St. Peter.

Your Date / Dogma list is a complete distortion of what we believe. The only reason this list makes sense to you is because, like all other Protestants, you reject Oral Tradition that has been passed down by word of mouth from pope to pope, bishop to bishop, and priest to priest. The first followers of Jesus were *Catholic Christians*.

. . . please don't distort what we believe as Catholics.

If you are unsure what we believe, ask us, not Andy anti-Catholic."

They ignored my points, and claimed the date / dogma list is a complete distortion of what they believe, yet the list of dogmas and dates came from their own *Catholic Encyclopedia!*

My reply:

"Thanks again for replying with more information this second time.

The simple answer of who you worship is very important to anyone, as you can well imagine.

I'm asking a Catholic, not an anti-Catholic, and I hope the whole team will get involved to provide a straight, simple answer to the two simple questions:

1. Who do you worship (obey).

2. What do you practice that proves that you worship (obey) who you say you do.

To a Catholic, the Catholic dogmas matter, since they are "dogmatic" and unalterable even by later dogmas.

I only presented them because they greatly add and take away from the Word of Yahuah, and emphasize obeying (worshipping) traditions of men. We are to *"live by every Word that proceeds from the mouth of Yahuah,"* not by men's words or traditions.

Traditions, rather than living according to Torah, was the big problem Yahusha had with the Pharisees, Sadducees, and the whole Sanhedrin.

There is no **oral tradition** recognized by Scripture (including the Talmud), only the unalterable written Word of Yahuah, or "Living Words," as stated at Acts 7:38.

The list of dogmas are from the Catholic encyclopedia, and are a timeline of required Catholic beliefs.

If any Catholic refuses to belief any one of them, they face excommunication by the terms of that faith group (not mine).

If you worship a deity, Jesus, what proof is there in how you live from what He said to do and obey?

We are to walk as He walked (live as He lived).

No doubt you know there was no one named "Jesus" in the first century, and you mean Yahusha (the only Name given).

The IESV, IHS, IES, IC-XC, and IESOUS Greco-Latin christograms and theonyms were devices to conceal the true Name, not reveal it.

If you worship Him, then everything He ordered must be obeyed. He said to "pray your flight is not in winter, or on the Shabath."

He did not mean the day of the Sun; Constantine altered the day of rest, and Laodicea outlawed resting on the 7th day.

If all the popes, bishops, and priests agreed on error, Yahusha's Word trumps them all.

Their words will pass away, Yahusha's Words will never pass away.

We are to *"live by every Word that proceeds from the mouth of Yahuah,"* not by men's words or traditions.

In reality, from everything you've said so far, **you worship tradition**, not the Creator, Yahusha. Perhaps I was misunderstood.

What is it that Catholics do that proves they worship Yahusha? No one knew anyone named Jesus until the 17th century on planet Earth. Please explain where Yahusha told us to get busy with ideas like Purgatory, eternal suffering in fire, relic kissing (veneration of human remains), transubstantiation (bread wafer transforms into living body and blood of Yahusha with words "hoc est corpus meum"), statue veneration (kneeling before objects), steeples/sun pillars, bells, worship of the "host" (in a monstrance – sun burst object), prayers to the dead (necromancy via rosaries), monks, nuns, popes, priests, celibacy, indulgences, trinity doctrine, infant baptism, apostolic succession, sacraments, crosses (symbol of Sun deity everywhere throughout history), replacement of Name Yahuah to "LORD" (Baal), adoption of Easter / Ishtar fertility festival with sunrise worship & egg/bunny/fish symbols, Natalis Sol Invictus (Saturnalia) transformed into "Christ-Mass," a celebration Yahusha's birth, - and much more."

HEBREW ROOTS ARE FEARED

Natsarim are feared by Christian leadership. Deep down, the Christian teachers know this: *their traditions will not survive the Second Coming.* The basic difference between the Natsarim and the Christians is not well understood. They adhere to two different things.

Christians practice (obey, serve, worship) **tradition**, while being told they "live by every Word that proceeds from the mouth of Yahuah." In fact, they observe nothing Yahuah commanded, and follow the previous traditions of cultures that worshipped the host of heaven (Babel's harlotry, Astrology).

Birthdays, Easter, Christmas, and so many other so-called "secular" practices originate from Babel's witchcraft, now considered cleansed of their former polluted fertility meaning because they are now directed at the worship of "Jesus." This is a *strong delusion*, since men's traditions will not survive the Second Coming.

When Yahusha comes back, the reign of Babel will have been swept away. No one will be saying, *"what's your sign?"* They will never hear *"I having a birthday party, can you come to it?"* There will be no more Christmas, Santa, tree-decorating, wreath-hanging, Easter bunny, colored eggs, Valentines Day hearts with arrows, tooth fairy, Halloween, or any other arrogant nonsense.

The original followers of Yahusha were called Natsarim (Acts 24:5). In the early centuries after Yahusha ascended, a blending of various Sun-worshipping consortiums took place at Alexandria, Egypt. Today we call them **church fathers**, and their teachings form the **Didache**. Their early name was the **Didascalia** (Greek, *"teaching authority"*), and later the "Catechetical Schola" (Latin, "echo-teaching school"). Responsatorial teaching was a technique developed to quickly train new adherents. The culture embraced all the traditions of paganism, while *leaving out the pattern of living taught and followed by Yahusha and His Natsarim.* The head masters of the Didascalia wrote of the Natsarim, calling them "heretics" because they did not conform to or recognize the teaching authority of the Catechetical School at Alexandria. Epiphanius (a church father) described Natsarim as living by the same customs as the Jews, only they believed in IESV (their name for Yahusha). He described how the Natsarim held a copy of the gospel of MatithYahu in the "Hebrew script" as it was "originally written." Jerome met one of the Natsarim and wrote about them also. Instead of worshipping traditions of men, Natsarim hold to the witness of Yahusha, and obey the Commandments (as written) of Yahuah. We preserve His Name, and His Word. The Latin word for **Didascalia** (teaching authority) is **Magisterium**.

The Magisterium controls much of what everyone believes, and this is accomplished by slowly **training people what to think from infancy**.

**WE'RE TRAINED TO OBEY TRADITION, AND DISOBEY YAHUAH
JUST AS NIMROD INTENDED FROM THE BEGINNING**

Nimrod's Star Religion Is All About Men's Traditions

The Didascalia (teaching authority) at Alexandria didn't understand the memo of the dividing wall being taken away, but put up one of its own. The Torah is for everyone (Ecc. 12:13), but men's traditions are not. Men's traditions will not survive the Second Coming.

Instead of living by every Word that proceeds from the mouth of Yahuah, we are taught to obey men's traditions instead, forsaking the Commandments of Yahuah. Let's ingraft into the original fig tree, and stop listening to the arrogant nonsense of men's traditions (**leaven**, yeast). See the topic **Matsah** near the end of this book.

Nimrod's World Order will not be happy about our decision, which is why family members are the first to notice a huge change in the things we do and don't do anymore.

The beast (reign of Babel) is an authoritarian slave master basing family bonds on birthdays, Christmas, Easter, Halloween, Sun-day, Valentine's Day - all of which are about fertility and Astrology (witchcraft). Yahuah's people are called to love Yahuah and one another by guarding the Ten Commandments, our marriage vows. The dragon hates this marriage, and so teaches everyone "those Commandments are not for you, we are not under the law."

We are called to repent and obey the Commandments of Yahuah, and forsake the commandments of men. When Yahusha returns, the "Them or Us" problem will vaporize.

Here's why the Ten Commandments matter:

"Blessed are those doing His commands, so that the authority

shall be theirs unto the tree of life, and to enter through the gates into the city. But outside are the dogs and those who enchant with drugs, and those who whore, and the murderers, and the idolaters, and all who love and do falsehood." -Rev. 22:14-15

CALENDAR SPECIALISTS

Private interpretations are often a cause for division and strife. Many modern teachers of "religion" have very little general knowledge of the "host of heaven," or how the universe actually operates.

All the **calendar specialists** we see appearing today use their private interpretations to explain their various methods of identifying the years, moons, or days, and they invent terms like Creation Calendar, Agriculturally-adjusted Calendar, Enochian Calendar, and generally put-down the Orthodox Jewish Calendar. Some have counted as many as 18 different "Messianic" approaches to setting the appointments of Yahuah, most using the "sighted moon" to determine the arrival of a New Moon. This idea was brought in by Anan in 767, as he was imprisoned to be executed by an Islamic Caliph in Babylon. By adopting the sighted moon, Anan managed to convince the Caliph his "religion" was different from the rest of the Yahudim, and so his life was spared. Yahudah and Afraim will join together into one stick, but some resist coming together in love. When a person reads the book of Enoch, they fail to recognize the difference between Sidereal time and Solar time. A Sidereal day is shorter than a Solar day, and the books of Enoch were written before the Great Flood. The Earth was altered in many ways at the time of the Great Flood. Babylonians estimated a year to be 360 days (approximately), giving us our 360-degrees in a circle.

Someone asked how the ancient Hebrews knew when the New Moon arrived without seeing it.

When the moon comes directly between the Earth and the Sun, the moon is at zero-light, and immediately begins to build the first day's light on it. When the moon has moved into a position where we can detect that light, we can see the fully built first day.

How did they determine the conjunction? They simply counted the days of the moon just as we do, although the Roman counting of days does not use the moon at all, and the number of days varies.

Daud and his best friend knew "tomorrow" would be the New Moon:

"So Yahunathan said to him, 'Tomorrow is the New Moon, and you shall be missed, because your seat shall be empty.'"

- 1 Sam. 20:18

Yahusha gave us sound advice concerning another kind of "watching" rather than "counting."

We observe the signs of budding plants, and follow these signs to know when summer is near. Beware of false teachers.

Mark 13:28 "And learn this parable from the fig tree: When its branch has already become tender, and puts forth leaves, you know that the summer is near."

We should not try to calculate when Yahusha will return, but watch for Him as a waiting bride, keeping our lamps lit. His delay is to give us time to work at gathering more people into His Covenant of love.

How Did One Faith Become Two Completely Different Ones?

Yahusha makes this statement at Mt. 4:4:

"'It has been written, "Man shall not live by bread alone, but by every word that comes from the mouth of Yahuah."'"

How can Yahusha's words be reconciled with what we've been taught? People are eating pigs, bowing to images of crosses, fixing Easter egg baskets, putting trees in their homes on December 25th, using steeples to indicate a worship building, dressing-up like Hindu priests and pretending to change bread and wine into Yahusha's body and splashing "holy water" on people, and generally doing all kinds of things without any notion of their pagan origins.

Yahusha is the Master of the Shabath (Sabbath), but Constantine transferred it, and the council of Laodicea (365/370 CE) declared all those who rested on the Sabbath "Judaizers," and "anathema."

If Yahusha is **Master of the Shabath** (and Yahuah does not change), **is His behavior now "anathema?"**

Yahusha said His Words would **"never pass away."**

How did we come to practice everything Yahuah told us not to practice (which pagans were doing), and not practice a single thing He told us to practice? While these things are blatantly obvious,

why is it that so few seem to be awake enough to notice?
What is His Name, and what is His Word?

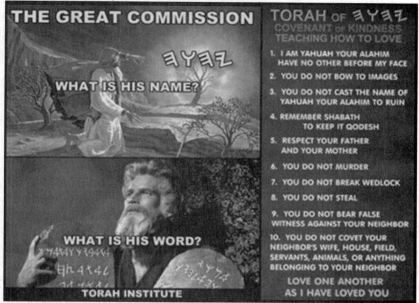

"So Yahusha said to those Yahudim who believed Him,
'If you stay in My Word, you are truly My taught ones, and you
shall know the Truth, and the Truth shall make you free.'" Yn. 8:31-32

THIS IS NOT A MICROPHONE TO SPEAK TO YAHUSHA:

Nearly one billion people follow a teaching authority guiding them to
commit gross acts of idolatry by deceiving them. A priest can not
change bread into anything other than what it is. He cannot forgive
anyone's sins, even his own! Only our Creator can forgive our sins.

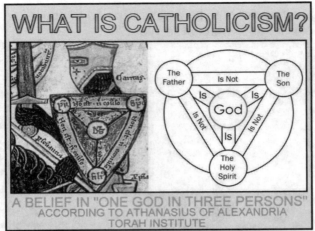

Is Yahuah Bitheistic, Trinitarian, Or One Being?

Dualism can be the belief in two opposing forces, such as good and evil. The Yin-Yang symbol of Gnosticism symbolizes this by teaching the physical reality is corrupt, while the non-physical reality is perfect. This sums up Gnosticism, and is the infiltration of eastern thought.

In the case of the belief in two beings as co-creators, the label dualism (or bitheism) seems to work for many believers.

Very early, a man named **Marcion** (85-160) taught that there were two deities, and that the Father was cruel while the Son was kind and became dominant. This is called **Marcionism**.

If a human being has two personalities, we call it schizophrenia. There is another possibility that is usually dismissed as heresy:

If a person understands that Yahuah became flesh, and we call on Him as Yahusha (meaning "I am your Deliverer"), it is only Yahusha that can reveal this to them. Most people do not know this because it has not been revealed to them.

"All have been handed over to Me by My Father, and no one knows the Son except the Father. Nor does anyone know the Father except the Son, and he to whom the Son wishes to reveal Him." – Mt. 11:27

Some have been led to think Yahuah is three yet one through programming (indoctrinating). A strawman is constructed by saying we are created as three components: mind-body-spirit, or body-soul-spirit. Tradition is a very powerful stronghold. Yahusha acknowledged only two components; a body and a nefesh. He said we should not fear the one that can destroy only the body:

"And do not fear those who kill the body but are unable to kill the being. But rather fear Him who is able to destroy both being and body in Gehenna." - Mt. 10:28

The word "both" is the key to this enigma. According to Yahusha, we are made up of a being (nefesh) and a physical body.

Athanasius of Alexandria consulted with Constantine at Nicea to write the Nicene Creed, setting forth Trinitarianism as the defining element of Catholicism.

Yahuah tells us there is no deliverer but Him, and Yahusha means, "I am your Deliverer." The prophet YashaYahu (Isaiah) speaks in His Name in chapters 43 and 45, revealing the Truth that there is no one beside Him. Note this statement carefully: **"Declare and bring near, let them even take counsel together. Who has announced this from of old? Who has declared it from that time? Is it not I, Yahuah? And there is no mighty one besides Me, a righteous Al and Deliverer, there is none besides Me."** - Isa / YashaYahu 45:21

SIGN OF THE EVERLASTING COVENANT: CHANGED?

What Day Is The Shabath? Speaking of the last days and the great distress at Mt. 24:20, Yahusha told His pupils who would be alive during the Day of Yahuah **"And pray that your flight does not take place in winter or on the Shabath."**

The weekly Shabath is the only day blessed by Yahuah, and He states it is a sign forever between Him and His people "forever." How can men transfer or alter this?

The Catholic dogma is that the resurrection of Yahusha is the basis for the transference of the day of rest to the first day, but that is a deception to remove the sign of the everlasting Covenant, and adopt the sign of Sun-day, Sun worship's special day.

First-fruits (one of the 7 high days) had always been a shadow of redemption, and Yahusha full-filled it by becoming the First-fruits which the wave sheaf offering pointed to.

In approximately 365-370 CE, the Council of Laodicea outlawed Shabath, and pronounced anathema-status on any who obeyed the 4th Commandment: **"Christians must not Judaize by resting on the Sabbath, but must work on that day, rather honoring the Lord's Day; and, if they can, resting then as Christians. But if any shall be found to be Judaizers, let them be anathema from Christ."**

Yahusha's reference at Mt. 24:20 has been falsely interpreted by preterists, but read His Word again from Mt. 24:20-21:

"And pray that your flight does not take place in winter or on the Shabath. For then there shall be great distress, such as has not been since the beginning of the world until this time, no, nor ever shall be."

The Catholic doctrine, followed by Protestants, is in direct conflict on this point, and endangers everyone misled by it. Constantine's

Christianity would in his words, **"have nothing in common with the hostile rabble of the Yahudim."** They share nothing in common. The Circus fathers made sure of this, and today Christians obey the Circus councils rather than have anything in common with Yahusha's walk, or any of His moral teachings or cultural patterns, except tithing. How easy it would have been if we had only been taught to obey the Torah! The reapers will remove all things offensive, then gather the wheat into the New Yerushalayim at Yahusha's coming. Even if we are united in error, we will perish. The "Living Word" is the Word we are to "live" in, and any other word is off the path of life, and not walking as Yahusha walked. Most people still don't even know His Name.

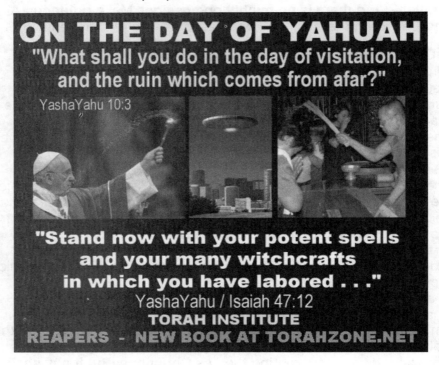

THE DAY OF VISITATION
Are you sealed for the day of redemption?
The coming of the seraphim on the Day of Yahuah will be the scariest day in all of human history. Messengers will be unleashed, and they will protect those who are sealed from being harmed.
The "burning ones," or seraphim, will first remove the weeds, then gather the elect for the wedding supper of the Lamb. The Day of Yahuah is explained by Scripture so everyone can understand the importance of repenting before the trap closes on them. The pre-Tribulation Rapture teaching is widely believed by those on the broad

road, but they are misled by its false promises.
The Name of Yahusha seals us for the day of redemption.
Everyone needs to prepare now, because the day comes quickly.

MARRIAGE

Is a marriage a covenant between a man and woman, pledging to serve one another until one of them dies? Absolutely, yes.
Who is the power of marriage vested in? The truth is so bizarre compared with what we are conditioned to think marriage is, it will seem completely inappropriate at first glance. Religious authorities, and governments, act in very similar ways. Yahuah brings a man and woman together, and any other power that attempts to encroach on His authority is a prop, or hoax - but people believe other authorities are real. The first man and woman had no ceremony; Yahuah brought the ashah to Adam, and they became one flesh. Yahuah was very much involved, and Yahusha mentioned how He made them male and female (Mt. 19:4-6). When Yitshaq and Rebekah became man and wife, Abraham wasn't present. How did they manage it?
Rebekah's brother and mother accepted the proposal from Abraham's servant Alazar, and then Rebekah accepted, even before meeting Yitshaq. There may or may not be a celebration party (such as the celebration we read of about the wedding at Kana), which today is called a reception. Some celebrations might last many days. But, in the case of Yitshaq and Rebekah, look at how the two became man and wife: "And Yitshaq brought her into his mother Sarah's tent. And he took Rebekah and she became his wife, and he loved her. Thus Yitshaq was comforted after his mother's death." - Gen / Barashith 24:67
This strikes at the heart of the artificial powers claimed by religious and state authorities, and the shallowness of engagement / wedding rings, wedding gowns, ceremonies, long engagement periods, and all other human traditions that strangle young couples. Everyone is so confused, people don't even know they're married when they live together as a married couple does. They are married, and a ceremony doesn't make them any more married than they already are. We have been looking at things only from our fleshly viewpoint for far too long. Yahuah brings us together, and no one else.

The Covenant Is a Marriage

The Creator has sent ambassadors into the world to call out to His bride.
The Covenant, the Ten Commandments, is a marriage agreement between Yahuah and all who are called to join to Him.
Most people read their favorite translation of Yahuah's Word for years, and never see the most glaring facts staring right at them. The Truth is,

39

Yahuah has never forsaken His Covenant with Yisharal (Israel), but has renewed it in the precious blood of Yahusha. Gentiles have been misled to think that He has given up on the people He Covenanted with, or that He made a "new" Covenant with a different people.
This is the core of what is called **replacement theology**, and it is a profound error (see Jer. 31:37). The Everlasting Covenant is with all who will receive it, and we are engrafted into the commonwealth of Yisharal through this Covenant.
We are "cut-off" from Yisharal the moment we depart from it. It is the renewal of this Covenant that is significant because it is sealed, not with the imperfect blood of rams and goats, but with the infinitely superior blood of the Son of Yahuah, Yahusha ha'Mashiak.
Yahusha is the Mediator of the renewed Covenant. He writes it upon hearts of flesh, and causes us to receive a love for the Truth.
He circumcises our hearts enabling us to love His instructions!
They show us how to love Him and our fellow creatures.
Gentiles become fellow citizens with Yisharal through this Covenant, and are referred to as being "formerly Gentiles in the flesh."
They are no longer Gentiles, but fellow citizens within Yisharal through the workmanship of Yahusha.
If we accept the Mashiak of Yisharal, but do not accept the Covenant He brings with Him, we are without hope, because of our disobedience. (See: Eph. 2:10-22, Heb. 4:6)
Yisharal is now the living Hekel (Temple) of Yahuah, indwelled by Yahusha's Spiritual presence in us. It has always been Yahuah's will for Yisharal to teach His Torah to the nations. The account of Yunah portrays Yisharal's unwillingness to perform this duty willingly, but now we in the last days realize our duty. We are commissioned to teach the gentiles, and engraft them into the Torah/Covenant (marriage); "teaching them to obey everything I have commanded you."
We are one body, and we have been called to be His bride: Yisharal.

(See more on Passover, First-fruits and the Resurrection as it relates to the sign of Yunah in the book **Fossilized Customs** by this author).

HOMOPHOBIA IS A MISNOMER

When the truth of anything comes out, the world reacts through the 3 stages:
1. It sounds ridiculous; 2. It is violently opposed; 3. It is accepted as being self-evident. **Homophobic** means "fear of one's same gender."
Acrophobia means "fear of heights."
The root cause of homosexual behavior is due to being "heterophobic" - a fear of the opposite gender. It is societal conditioning, not a disease or one's "orientation."

The sons of Aharon who became the kohenim (priesthood) were the butchers/chefs for atonement operations, and they served as the medical staff for the nation.

Imagine, for a moment, after one of these priests helped a man determine if a boil on his skin was unclean, another person comes up with his problem.

The man sits down and tells the priest,

"I think I have some kind of disease."

"What seems to be the trouble?" asks the priest.

"I'm sexually aroused whenever I'm around young boys" says the man.

The priest pauses and thinks for a moment, then says,

"Yes, you may have a disease of some kind. Perhaps it would be best, for now, if you avoided being around any young boys."

Yahuah is the same yesterday, today, and forever, and He does not change.

Perversion, or an abomination, is not a disease; it's a decision to rebel. Improper use of Yahuah's creation will bring judgment.

Sodom is all around us, and the reapers are coming soon.

Openly gay men are now officially acceptable to be scout leaders.

This is like putting a fox in charge of a hen house.

"And a man who lies with a male as he lies with a woman: both of them have done an abomination, they shall certainly be put to death, their blood is upon them." - Lev / Uyiqra 20:13

The above Scripture, and others pertaining to this subject, will be the reason the Scriptures will come under attack. Our enemy is not flesh and blood.

Yahuah does not recognize two men or two women to be a marriage, because it is He who said: (note the terms "male" and "female" in this text):

"And He answering, said to them, "Did you not read that He who made them at the beginning made them male and female, and said, 'For this cause a man shall leave his father and mother and cleave to his wife, and the two shall become one flesh'?

So that they are no longer two, but one flesh. Therefore, what Alahim has joined together, let man not separate." - Mt. 19:4-6

We know who it is that hates marriage: satan.

The one who tells the truth comes under attack, and the wrong are cheered and paraded in the streets. When the Sun goes dark, and the moon turns blood-red, the wrong will then have something to fear.

They will be *"Yahushaphobic"* - and the winepress of the wrath of Yahuah will be filled on the Day of Yahuah.

"Do not make idols for yourselves and do not set up
a carved image or a pillar for yourselves, and do not place
a stone image in your land, to bow down to it. For I am Yahuah your Alahim."

ONLY YAHUSHA CAN RESTORE EYESIGHT TO THE BLIND
RECEIVE YAHUSHA'S TORAHVISION
HE IS OUR ONLY TEACHING AUTHORITY

Yahusha's Mind inhabits those who belong to Him, and He shares His
Torahvision with their hearts (thoughts), seeing things as He see them.
With His Mind in you, can you see and understand His thoughts,
knowing He does not change, shift, or blend light and darkness?
Yahusha's thoughts are what we mean by "Torahvision."
His thoughts, or Torahvision, is the Mind of the Spirit.

DEIFICATION RITUAL - ROME   LUXOR EGYPT

The Vatican Museum preserves the images of the pagan world,
yet Yahuah told us to smash their pillars and remove the names
of their deities. How faithful to Him have men been?

UNCOVERING THE NAKEDNESS; THE BALLS (TESTICLES), TINSEL (SEMEN), AND RIBBONS (HYMEN)

PILLAR OF JEALOUSY EZ 8 — ASHERAH — MAYPOLE WITH WREATH

THE ERECT POLE, HAT, TREE, OR SPIRE ARE HIDDEN SYMBOLS OF MALE FERTILITY
THE PHALLUS, AND THE ACCOMPANYING VAGINA, THE WREATH, ARE DETESTABLE

WHAT IS THE NAME ABOVE ALL NAMES?

We have an identity crisis. People encountering the Hebrew (and only true Name) of our Master automatically say "He knows my heart, it doesn't matter what we call Him." If only they could support this kind of thinking with some Scripture texts teaching this idea. Yahuah says He is jealous, and gave examples of how they stopped using His Name, but called on BAAL (LORD) instead (see YirmeYahu 23:26). Look at this text of YashaYahu (Isaiah):

"I am Yahuah, that is My Name, and My esteem I do not give to another, nor My praise to idols." – YashaYahu 42:8

The true Name is a serious threat to tradition, so we see a growing resistance to it in those demonizing the "Hebrew Roots."
Ignorance is a choice in the Information Age.
The true Name is spreading rapidly among many new Natsarim.
At the same time, new errors are being invented by those who have little information about Hebrew, and those who don't know the language was attacked to keep everyone from pronouncing the Name correctly.
The Masoretes fouled the vowels, causing the letter ALEF to be treated as "E," and the letter UAU to be an "O" rather than a U.
YAHU became YEHO, influencing all transliterations from the KJV forward.
The myth that Hebrew "has no written vowels" is a lie. The Name is written with four vowels. The Hebrew vowels are ALEF, AYIN, YOD, UAU, HAY. These became our modern A, E, I, U/O.
The lack of the letters "J" and "W" (double-U) in Hebrew, Greek, and Latin are being discovered by large numbers of people.
Variances of transliterating the four vowels yod-hay-uau-hay will continue, so we have to be tenderhearted with all those who understand differently. The Hebrew letter UAU became the Greek Upsilon, and then went into the Latin. *UPSILON* is our letter U.

43

The Latin shape for U is "V" – and in the 1400's this developed into a double "V" (VV) because a clever typesetter combined two letters into one piece of type, creating the letter "double-U."
One of the refinements is to correct the error of all those using the "W" in transliteration, and going with the one letter, U.
HallelU-Yah is not hallelW-Yah, neither is YAHUDAH to be YahWudah. YAHUAH and YAHUSHA are the simplest transliterations, and should be what the next generation inherits from us.

The Hebrew name **Michal** is *Michael* in Greek - G3413; **Danial** *is Daniel* - G1158; **Adam** is *Adam* - G76; even **shatan** is *satanas* - G4567; but **IESV** shows up in our KJV in place of the real Name. Later, the KJV altered IESV to JESUS.
No one ever laid eyes on the word **JESUS** until the 17th century. What's that about?
Some pastors are speaking to their congregations about this, being dumbfounded about the deception and saying so. Others rail against those teaching the **Hebrew Roots** of our faith.
If the correct Hebrew Name for our Deliverer is **Yahusha**, how can it be some other Name **"in English?"** Obviously, only false teachers would teach another name.
How can we recognize a false teacher? They teach things Yahuah did not speak about, and instead bear down with things men invented. They use languages to misdirect, knowing that most of their victims don't know the difference between translating and transliterating.
The Pharisees never knew of anyone named Jesus.
I'm only pointing out what is overwhelmingly obvious, and sharing Light - I was once blind also. The reason the Name was taken from the lips of Yahuah's people is because **they would not obey Him**. As long as we will not obey Him, He will not allow us to call on His Name either. YashaYahu / Is. 8:20 shows us how to recognize a false teacher. Which of Yahuah's Ten Commandments can you read at Exodus (Shemoth) 20, and honestly say it is practiced? If we don't practice them, then a false teacher has influenced us to disregard (annul) those we fail to abide in. If we abide in Yahusha's Word (and He is Yahuah, our Deliverer), then we are truly His pupils, and we will know the Truth (His Word), and the Truth will set us free.

OUR MIND OF THE FLESH IS NARCISISTIC
A narcissist is a person who is preoccupied with their own prestige,

and has little or no concern for anyone or anything else. It is a personality disorder, and yet it is also common to all of us. Scripture calls it the "mind of the flesh." We are all blind until we are given sight by Yahusha.

When Yahusha shares His Mind with us, we see His purposes and we can overcome our fleshly point-of-view. We are all narcissistic to some extent. The instruction of Yahuah (Torah) teaches us how to love Him in the first 4 directives, and how to love our fellow human beings in the last 6 directives. When we fail to do them, we fail to love.

Which of the Ten Commandments is the most disgusting directive to you?

OBEDIENT ONES ARE THE NATSARIM COUNTERCULTURE
Counterculture definition:
Noun: *a way of life and set of attitudes opposed to or at variance with the prevailing social norm.*

Yahusha will instill His Spirit in those who will submit to His will. He will give them His Torahvision, the ability to see His heart's perspective of how we walk (live, behave).

Yahusha and His pupils were the counterculture of His day. He was not rebellious against Torah, but against the Establishment's failure to live by Torah. They were living out and practicing men's traditions, not the instructions of Yahuah which teach us love.

THE WITNESS OF YAHUSHA

About 2,000 years ago, a message, or testimony was given to some average men to share with every nation, tribe, and language across this planet. The message was so powerful it was attacked by an enemy whose estate is in the spiritual dimension, a higher plane than mortals can perceive. In this higher plane there is a war being waged to dominate the minds of mankind. Your mind is part of this war's battlefield. The message has been corrupted so badly it is rarely heard. **All those who are gainfully employed to proclaim it have no clue what the message is.**

"To the Torah and to the witness! If they do not speak according to this Word, it is because they have no light of dawn."
- (Isa) YashaYahu 8:20 ʙʏɴᴠ (BYNV available at torahzone.net)

Yahusha's witness is also known as the **Great Commission**. The final word, or end of the matter (Eccl. 12:13) is to obey the Commandments of Yahuah. They teach us love, and are the Living Words to be written on every heart. This Covenant of lovingkindness is the bond of marriage between us and Yahuah. The enemy hates it. The Day of Yahuah is also called the Day of Yahusha. Psalm 91

45

describes judgment day, the time the seraphim (reapers) are sent to reap the grapes (consigned for wrath). They will have been appointed to guard us in all our ways, and not let us even so much as stub our toe ("dash your foot against a stone" – verse 12).

THE ENEMY WILL BE REMOVED FROM REIGNING
Many unbelievers blame Yahuah for all the suffering in the world, but it will be shown (at the end) it was the enemy that brought the first lie into the world, and continues to deceive mankind.
Some atheists hold to their atheism because they are angry at Yahuah, but it is the enemy they should be blaming. The enemy is called "a man" in the following text, meaning "person." This enemy will be put on display as the perpetrator, and held in a pit for a time of final destruction of all those who rebelled against Yahuah.
YashaYahu / Is. 14:16-20:
"Those who see you stare at you, and ponder over you, saying, 'Is this the man who made the Earth tremble, who shook reigns, who made the world as a wilderness and destroyed its cities, who would not open the house of his prisoners?'
All the sovereigns of the gentiles, all of them, were laid in esteem, everyone in his own house; but you have been thrown from your grave like an abominable branch, like the garment of those who are slain, thrust through with a sword, who go down to the stones of the pit, like a trampled corpse.
You are not joined with them in burial, for you have destroyed your land and slain your people. Let the seed of evil-doers never be mentioned."
THE SIMPLE TRUTH - From Yahusha's Point Of View
Yahuah the Creator humbled Himself in the extreme by coming to us in human form to speak to us (Heb. 1:1-4).
He showed us perfect love in the way He lived. Then He showed us ultimate love by shedding His blood for all mankind.
He demonstrated how we are to live. We are to walk as He walked. Love is expressed to Yahuah in the first 4 Commandments, and love for our fellow beings in the last 6 Commandments.
He came in His Father's Name: Yah (see Psalm 68:4, Prov. 30:4). The only name given among men by which we must be delivered is Yahusha, meaning "I am (Yah) your Deliverer (sha)."
Jesus is not the name He came in, this was inherited from the Latin Vulgate's IESV, taken into the KJV as IESV, and altered later to IESUS in subsequent printings. There was no cross, only a STAUROS (stake, pole). Jerome translated the word **STAUROS** from the Greek into **CRUX** in the 4th century, and ignored the matching Latin word STAURO (stake, pole).

46

The symbol of the cross is the most ancient symbol for the Sun, which Constantine worshipped as Apollo (Sol Invictus).

The Pharisees of Yahusha's day never knew anyone named "Jesus." The reason so many of Yahusha's own people have resisted believing in Him is they don't know what to think of the name, "Jesus."

I've had visitors from Israel speak with me in person about this issue, and they feel that if the Christians can't get His Name right, they are uneasy about listening to anything else they may have to say about their beliefs. Also, they see they have altered the day of rest to the pagan day of the Sun, and they eat unclean animals.

Only the most unstable among them would convert to Christianity.

The original followers called themselves "Natsarim" (Acts 24:5).

This word means "branches" (of His teachings), and also means **watchmen**. This is because we are **guardians** of His **Name** and His **Word**. Long ago we were called Christianos by outsiders. This was a Greek term of scorn, and in that day meant *cretin* or *idiot*. Look up the word **cretin** and you'll see it is originally derived directly from the Greek term, **Christianos**.

This information is only a threat to tradition, as Truth always is.

When we change our perspective from Nimrod's to Yahuah's, we see and hear correctly. Until we do this, ***it's all Nimrod, all the time.***"

COME TO THE LIGHT

YashaYahu / Isa 8:20: **To the Torah and to the witness! If they do not speak according to this Word, it is because they have no daybreak.**" Yahusha is the Living Word of Yahuah, the Light of the world. Without knowing what the Light or Word is, we will continue to walk (conduct ourselves, behave) in "darkness." Yahuah's Torah is

Light, a lamp that shows us the way: **"Your word is a lamp to my feet And a light to my path."** - Psa 119:105

"My son, watch over your father's command, And do not forsake the Torah of your mother. Bind them on your heart always; Tie them around your neck. When you are walking about, it leads you; When you lie down, it guards you. And when you have woken up, It talks to you. For the command is a lamp, And the Torah a light, And reproofs of discipline a way of life, To guard you against an evil woman, From the flattering tongue of a strange woman." – Proverbs 6:20-24

Proverbs 3 tells us wisdom is Torah, the instructions of Yahuah. This Torah is personified as a *she*, and is also referred to as the *Tree of Life*. At Proverbs 8, we glean much more about Torah.

"By me sovereigns reign, and rulers make righteous decrees. By me princes rule, and nobles, all the judges of the earth. I love those who love me, and those who earnestly seek me do find me." - Proverbs 8:15-17 *Do you love the Torah?*

"And now, listen to me, you children, for blessed are they who guard my ways. Listen to discipline and become wise, and do not refuse it. Blessed is the man who listens to me, watching daily at my gates, waiting at the posts of my doors. For whoever finds me shall find life, and obtain favor from Yahuah, But he who sins against me injures himself. All who hate me love death!" Pro 8:32-36

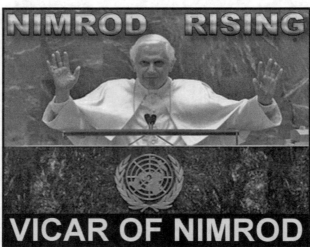

Vicar is a title meaning *"one in place of."* Since Nimrod became a mighty-one (deity), other rulers followed in his example. In the Roman Catholic Timeline on page 29, we see the holder of the office of the papacy is dogmatically proclaimed to be "LORD GOD."

WISDOM & THE MARK OF THE BEAST

Proverbs 1:6 tells us **wisdom _enables us to understand_** proverbs, figures of speech, **_and riddles._**

The _mark of the beast_ is a riddle, only solvable by having "wisdom." Wisdom is the knowledge of Torah, simply the Ten Commandments. Those who follow the beast (reign of Babel) don't know which day we are to rest, and not buy and sell. Figure it out if you have ears to hear (the Word of Yahuah).

The beast's mark is the ancient symbol and weekly conduct seen openly everywhere. The ancient Sun worshipers assembled on the Day of the Sun (Sun-day), in the morning, with a pillar (steeple), rang bells, and honored the symbol of the sun, the crux. These customs are not from Yahuah's Word, but Nimrod's worship of the host of heaven - witchcraft.

Yahuah's mark? The seventh day, which He blessed at creation. What are we to do? Stop and rest. Obedience is worship. We are servants of the one we obey (Romans 6:16).

RELIGION OF TRADITIONS

The Second Coming will wipe-clean the traditions and decisions of all the councils, and we will reboot to the Living Words of Yahuah only. Natsarim don't use any "sacraments," and our fellowship with Yahusha as our only Head and teaching authority is vastly different from the fourth beast's religion of traditions.

We simply teach the Commandments as written, and they shape hearts with Yahuah's will, and love is the outcome. Yahusha is in charge at all times, and no one gets burned, hung, or even judged.

We work among those who serve their religious traditions, but we don't observe those traditions.

We are free, because we live in Yahuah's Word, not men's traditions. You can wrestle with what men think, but the yoke (teachings) of Yahusha will set you free.

Religion is tradition; but knowing the will of Yahusha is reality, and produces the fruits of His Spirit. Arius was right, and persecuted by the Alexandrian Cult, but Natsarim don't argue about such things. The words of Athanasius will pass away, but the Word of Yahuah will remain forever.

Focus on "living by every Word that proceeds from the mouth of Yahuah," and surrender in humility to living by His instructions, and the heavy yoke of men's teachings will drop from your shoulders. I know what you're going through, I was trained by the Jesuit-Illuminati, and it messes with your ability to think properly. Yahusha (meaning "I am your Deliverer") can deliver you from all of it.

Call on His one, true Name, and stand still and watch how He delivers.

Then, your heart will break for those who are still blinded by Nimrod's plot, still active in the world as the Mother of Harlots.

If you want to stand before the Throne of the universe and explain your preference to live by a "non-legal" method, that's always a choice to be made. We are already non-legal, but moving in the direction of the Living Words (to live by) is not heretical or evil. We are ambassadors, as if Yahuah Himself is pleading with people to be restored to favor. If we pleaded with them to just believe and live under "grace" and to ignore the fact they are eating ham, working their job on the day we were told to rest, and calling Yahuah by whatever name tradition has taught us to call Him, we live in a delusion. Yahusha is the Living Word, and we are told to **"walk even as He walked."**
Those who do not live by the Commandments do not know Him, and do not belong to Him.
Unintentional sin (crime) is where "grace" applies. To sin intentionally, while knowing what is right but ignoring it, is where grace does not apply. Ask Yahusha how He wants you to live. If you live the way He wants, you will not fit into the **religion of tradition**, and will be shunned by everyone who wants to remain the way they are.

YOKE: A BODY OF TEACHINGS
Do we have freedom to disobey the Commandments and do the things Yahuah calls an abomination? No, of course not. Our freedom is from the *traditions of men*, which Yahusha was most critical of. Yahusha calls the teachings of men "**leaven**." He was not upset because they obeyed the Commandments, but rather because they disobeyed them and *made men's traditions their commandments.*
Here's the proof of this statement at Mt. 15:7-9:
"Hypocrites! YashaYahu (Isaiah) **rightly prophesied about you, saying, 'This people draw near to Me with their mouth, and respect Me with their lips, but their heart is far from Me.
But in vain** (futility) **do they worship Me, teaching as teachings the commands of men.' "**
What I'm about to describe will bring many teachers kicking and screaming out into the light: *A yoke is a body of teachings.*
The yoke described in Galatians, and Mt. 16, is men's traditions.
Most teachers misidentify the "yoke" being discussed, thinking it refers to the "Ten Commandments." This will explain what Paul was really referring to, which Catholics and Protestant teachers still twist:
PAUL'S FORMER WAY - Gal 1:13, 14:
"For you have heard of my former way of life in Yahudaism, how intensely I persecuted the body of Alahim, and ravaged it. And I

50

progressed in Yahudaism beyond many of my age in my race, being exceedingly ardent for the traditions of my fathers."

This YOKE was not the Torah of Mosheh; it was the traditions of the fathers. *Now we can understand what this means:*
Act 15:10: **"Now then, why do you try Alahim by putting a yoke on the neck of the taught ones which neither our fathers nor we were able to bear?"**
The yoke (teachings) of the *traditions of the fathers* was keeping men from calling on the Name of Yahuah. Traditions of men confuse us to act unwisely. The wisdom of men is falsely called knowledge. Gnosticism, mystical and allegorical interpretations, and all of Nimrod's influences originated outside the true faith.
"How is it that you do not understand that I did not speak to you concerning bread, but to beware of the leaven of the Pharisees and Sadducees?" Then they understood that He did not say to beware of the leaven of bread, but of the teaching of the Pharisees and the Sadducees." Mt. 16:11, 12

Question: What is the leaven, or yeast of the Pharisees?
Answer: Rabbinic Judaism, the traditions of the fathers.

WHAT THINGS DO WE REALLY OBEY?

People do not obey a single thing Yahuah told us to do, but instead live by traditions inherited from pagans. They do not live by every Word that proceeds from the mouth of Yahuah (Mt. 4:4).
This statement made by Yahusha is the focal point of His criticism of those leading His people. Being a teacher of Torah, rather than tradition, Yahusha was the counter-culture of that time. His Natsarim are now that same counter-culture, rejecting and exposing the teaching authority of our time.
When I first read Acts 4:12, the meaning of the verse jumped out at me. Scripture does not justify traditions and excuses for disobeying. Traditions have programmed us to keep doing things we want to do in defiance of Yahuah's Word. Mt. 4:4 tells us we do not live by bread only, but by every Word that proceeds from the mouth of Yahuah. While most call on what they think is His Name, I try to imitate Aquila and Priscilla by expounding on the Word of Yahuah more accurately. Mikal is Michael, Danial is Daniel, and shatan is satanas when we examine the Hebrew-to-Greek; yet the Name of our Deliverer is ravaged beyond recognition. Yahusha means "I am your Deliverer." What does Jesus mean? I've rung the bell most people would prefer to not have been rung, but the bottom line is what do we see taught that Yahuah instructed to be obeyed?

Yahuah tells us our teachers are blind, and the cause is given at YashaYahu (Is.) 8:20.

They don't teach or focus on the Commandments of love, but expect us to tithe to them? Why more people don't see this is a very curious thing. What exactly is
"every Word that proceeds from the mouth of Yahuah?"

SO WHAT SHOULD WE BE OBSERVING?
Redemption Plan - Hebrew Roots Research by Lew White
SEVEN REDEMPTIVE SHADOWS OF THE YEAR
Yahusha's redemption plan for His bride (Yisharal/Israel)
The symbol of the menorah, a tree of life and light to the world, pictures His seven assemblies in the branches, and Himself as the Root. The Plan of Redemption is not limited to being an "Old Testament" model. Yahusha Himself, as well as Peter and Paul, reveal the **Day of Judgment** (by fire) that is still ahead of us.

These shadows show us past and future redemptive events.
"I was in the Spirit on the Master's (kuriakos) **Day"** in order to reveal **future events** to the assemblies. It is only confusing because our slumbering teachers fumble with the meaning of words in their context. By not feeding the sheep **"every Word that proceeds from the mouth of Yahuah,"** the sheep remain unprepared for the day set by Yahuah to remove the weeds. The 10th day of the 7th moon will be our day of redemption, just as it was instituted by Yahuah to be. It will also be the day of termination by burning as we read about in Joel 2, Zeph.

1:14, Obad. 1:15, and Psalm 91.

The final warning is to **"Come out of her My people"** (Rev. 18:4) in order we not receive the plagues coming in the **end of days**.

Christians have been misled about the end of days. The message for the last days at Malaki 4:1-6: **"Remember the Torah of Mosheh."** It's confusing when you are taught to "not" live by every Word that proceeds from the mouth of Yahuah.

Shadow Of Things To Come?

Redemption Plan In The Festivals Of Yisharal (Israel)

Our redemption by Yahusha is outlined, or shadowed in the feasts. At Col. 2:17 we read of the "shadow of things to come." This has been poorly understood until these last days before the return of Yahusha. The redemption plan of Yahuah's people (which includes those formerly gentile persons engrafted by joining with Yahuah through the Covenant) is outlined (shadowed) in the annual appointments we are commanded to observe each year: the moedim.

These moedim are now understood to be REDEMPTIVE festivals that make use of agricultural symbols. As we observe them year after year, they teach us Yahusha's process and His involvement in our redemption.

Passover, **First-fruits**, **Matsah**, and **Shabuoth** have seen their fulfillment with Yahusha's first coming as the Lamb of Alahim (Passover), then He resurrected as First-fruits (Wave-Sheaf Offering), and finally indwelling His first followers (Natsarim, branches) to write the renewed Covenant on their hearts (and ours) at Shabuoth (Acts 2 & 3). Passover outlines how Yahusha's blood covers our crime against His Torah of love. Matsah (Unleavened Bread) removes the moldy, puffed-up teaching authority of men from our hearts, so our hearts are able to receive the teachings of Yahusha without the ideas of men corrupting them. First-fruits is about Yahusha's resurrecting from the dead, the First-fruits of all to be resurrected to eternal life. Shabuoth is the receiving of the Living Torah, Yahusha Himself, remembering the marriage Covenant given at Sinai, renewed in power by the indwelling of Yahusha's Spirit in His Natsarim.

AHEAD: THE UNFULFILLED SHADOWS
YOM TERUAH - YOM KAFAR - SUKKOTH

The final unfulfilled festivals of these agricultural metaphors concern the **harvest of the Earth**, and are shadowed in the appointed times in the 7th moon of each year.

The first day of the 7th moon, the day of the shout, **Yom Teruah**, foreshadows the resurrection of the First-fruits who have died and will be raised to life just prior to Yahusha returning to reign.

Then, on the 10th day (**Yom Kafar**), the reapers are released to destroy the unrighteous, all those not sealed with Yahusha's Name. All who are not sealed with His Name are not His property, so they are to be burned to ashes for their rebellion. This is judgment day, the fall of the reign of Babel. It is also the day of our redemption, when the reign is given to us, and we will reign with Yahusha for the next 1000 years on Earth in our immortal bodies.

Finally the wedding supper of the Lamb commences in the new Yerushalayim. The malakim gather us who remain (Natsarim sealed for protection, Ps. 91) from the ends of the Earth.

This is called **Sukkoth**, Tents, or Tabernacles.

If you watch The Reapers on youtube.com it will explain a great deal about the harvest festivals ahead of us. As the **Day of Yahuah** approaches, we need to comfort one another and all those around us with these words:

"Here is the endurance of the set-apart ones; here are those who are guarding the Commandments of Alahim and the belief of Yahusha." Unbelieving Yahudim or Christians cannot claim to be these "first-fruits" described in this verse at Rev 14:12, nor this verse:

"Blessed are those doing His Commands, so that the authority shall be theirs unto the tree of life and to enter through the gates into the city." - Rev 22:14

Scripture doesn't say, "Blessed are those practicing the Talmud." The Talmud did not exist in the days of Yahusha, Paul, Luke, and the rest of the Talmidim (students). It was in the form of the "oral law", the traditions of the elders, and Yahusha nor any of His followers had anything to do with it.

WHAT ABOUT THE ORAL LAW?

There is still a division over what some perceive as traditions "orally" handed-down. Every Word of Yahuah was written, and read aloud to the people. The oral instructions, or *traditions of the fathers,* was the paradigm Paul said was his **former way of** living by.

He called it **"Yahudaism."**

"For you have heard of my former way of life in Yahudaism, how intensely I persecuted the assembly of Alahim, and ravaged it." - see Gal 1:13. Note the phrase, "*former way of life.*"

This **"yoke"** (teaching authority) of men is described here:

"Now then, why do you try Alahim by putting a yoke on the neck of the taught ones which neither our fathers nor we were able to bear?" - Acts 15:10. The yoke of the *traditions of the fathers* (the leaven of men's teachings) Yahusha called "old wine."

The traditions of men are the object lesson from Matsah (Unleavened Bread). We must become unleavened, purging the teaching authorities and corrupting influences of men's ideas which block the pure and clean objective of love, which the Torah's goal is to teach us.

613 LAWS – WHAT, WHO, AND WHY

The 613 "laws" (directives) in Scripture pertain to not only different circumstances, but **who one is**. For example, Yahusha could not obey a directive that pertained only to females. Females could not obey a directive concerning only males. *Hundreds* of the directions were for the kohenim (priesthood) in their duties, most of which are impossible because Yahuah brought atonement through His Own flesh and blood. Even the hair control of the priesthood was directed. The priests had to keep their hair trimmed and wear a bonnet for hair control while in their services, but a regular guy, farmer, or a king, did not.

The Covenant (Ten Words) is for all men, for all time, and teaches us how to love. They are the **Living Word** (to "live" in). We are to speak of them when we rise up, lie down, sit, walk, go in and out. We are to teach them diligently to our offspring. Ecc. 12:13 tells us they are for all men, not just for certain people and circumstances. Pastors have failed us by obeying Constantine and the Circus fathers rather than Yahuah. Yahusha is Yahuah, and He is same yesterday, today, and forever. He's the One living inside you now, and can write a love for His Torah (instructions in love) on your heart (your thoughts, mind, inner lamp). When that happens, you are His follower, one of the Natsarim (branches of His teachings, a guardian of His Name and Word).

You move from the unwise to the wise virgin status, and will be of the higher-calling, His bride. The reapers will protect you as they remove the weeds from our midst on the Day of Yahusha, and they will not permit you to even stub your toe (dash your foot against a stone).

IS YAHUSHA YAHUAH? His Name reveals His Identity

Let's look at what He says about it.

YashaYahu 43:11 states:

"I, I am Yahuah, and besides Me there is no Deliverer."

YAHUAH: I WAS, I AM, I WILL BE
YAHUAH ALAHIM: I AM YOUR LOFTY ONE
YAHUAH RAFA: I AM YOUR HEALER
YAHUAH YIREH: I AM YOUR PROVIDER
YAHUAH ADONAI: I AM YOUR SOVEREIGN
YAHUAH AL SHADDAI: I AM MIGHTY OVERWHELMINGLY
YAHUAH SHALOM: I AM COMPLETENESS (PEACEFULNESS)
YAHUAH RO: I AM YOUR SHEPHERD
YAHUSHA: I AM YOUR DELIVERER

His identity has been hidden in countless controversial disputes, and it cannot be known unless it is revealed to you by Him:

Luke 10:22-24: "'**All has been delivered to Me by My Father, and no**

one knows <u>Who</u> the Son is, except the Father, and <u>Who</u> the Father is, except the Son, and he to whom the Son wishes to reveal Him.'
And turning to His taught ones He said, separately, 'Blessed are the eyes that see what you see, for I say to you that many prophets and sovereigns have wished to see what you see, and have not seen it, and to hear what you hear, and have not heard it.'"
Who the Son is, and Who the Father is remains unknown except to **"he to whom the Son wishes to reveal."** The greatest declaration of all, affirmed by Yahusha, is the Shema (Dt. 6:4), that Yahuah is one.

He is alone, and there is no other. He has become your Deliverer.

Yahuah's highest attribute concerns our redemption. Yahuah has become our Deliverer, and we call on Him as our Deliverer: YAHUSHA.

THE OLDEST LIE OF THEM ALL

Lies come in all shapes and sizes, and are right at the "tip of our tongue" at all times.
Some lies are so huge it has become heretical to oppose them.
One of those is the idea that the universe created itself.

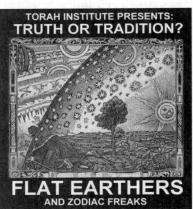

Here's The Oldest Lie Of Them All: "You Don't Have To Obey."
The old serpent lied. Nimrod was a superman, and the serpent logo is shown to us in plain sight, continuing to deify a human being:

The <u>Goal</u> of the Torah, Not the <u>End</u> of the Torah
"For I bear them witness that they have an ardour for Yahuah, but not according to knowledge. For not knowing the uprightness of Yahuah, and seeking to establish their own uprightness, they did not subject themselves to the uprightness of Yahuah.
For Mashiak is the goal of the Torah to uprightness to everyone who believes." - Romans 10:2-4 BYNV

The word "end" does not mean the "termination" of the Torah.
It means the objective purpose, ultimate conclusion, summation, completeness (shalom), and point of it all. Love is the goal, and Yahusha is love. The purpose of Torah is **<u>love</u>**. It is called "wisdom" and the "tree of life" in Proverbs. If Torah were to cease to exist, then wisdom and love would also cease to exist.

57

RESTORING A PURE LIP

LEXOMORPHOSIS - A belief that letters transform into other letters
Many teachers today have said there are "no written vowels in Hebrew." And yet, Yusef Ben MattithYahu (Flavius Josephus) wrote in the first century that he had seen the golden headpiece worn by the Kohen ha'Gadol, and he described how it was written in four vowels, in Hebrew (not the square Aramaic script we usually see called "modern Hebrew"). Clement of Alexandria transliterated the Name in Greek vowels, **IAOUE**.

The Greek vowels come directly from ancient Hebrew's written vowels, ALEF, AYIN, YOD, UAU (the last, UAU, written Y, became the Greek UPSILON, our letter U). The Latin inherited the UPSILON (shaped Y) and dropped the lower stem, so the letter appears as V (GLADIVS is actually pronounced "GLADIUS").   We write English in Latin letters. We understand the vowels are AEIOU, and sometimes Y and W. Some letters did not exist until recent centuries because they evolved from other letters. The letters J, W, and V have developed within the last 600 years.

The letter "double-U" (VV) is about 600 years old. As the printing press was developing, typesetters used the letter U, but it was shaped V from the Latin. When Old English words like VVITCH, VVICK, or VVHITE were printed, a shrewd typesetter invented a single piece of metal type using two V's side-by-side, and so the letter "double-U" was invented.

Modern Hebrew has inherited the corrupted influences of the Masoretes, a Karaite sect of traditionalists who abhorred anyone pronouncing the Name "YAHUAH" aloud. They invented vowel marks called NIQQUD to misdirect the sound of words. YAHU became YEHO, and ALAHIM became ELOHIM. ABRAHIM begins with an ALEF, and so does ALAHIM. The Arabs pronounce Hebrew words more accurately than modern Yahudim do. They name their children Ashah (not Ishah), Daud (not David), Yaqub (not Jacob), and refer to the Creator as ALAH (a pronoun, not a personal name). This is not to say their theology is correct, only their language.

Modern Hebrew inherited outsiders' distortions as well. The use of the so-called modern Hebrew letter "V" for the letter BETH, as well as the letter UAU, are examples. The phrase "HALLELU YAH" uses the letter UAU (same as the Greek UPSILON or our letter U). If we put the new letter sound we know as "V" into words, they become nonsense: YAHVAH, HALLELVYAH, YAHVDAH; the letters U, V, and W are next to one another in our "alphabetical" or "alefbethical" order, and the U produced the new letters V and W. Look up the history of the letters V and W, and prove to yourself these things are true.

Some of you may have noticed the anachronism of the Mosheh display at the Answers In Genesis Museum. The script the museum used on the tablets is **Aramaic**, not Hebrew. No reference to "Aramaic" is found in the Natsarim Writings, but the *Hebrew* language is described eleven times.

Most revisionist scholars like to promote the idea that the Natsarim wrote their memoirs in Greek, but even the Greek language in the mouth of Paul was quite shocking to the Roman officer (Acts 21:37).

My biggest criticism of the AIG museum is their handling of creation week. They skip the 7th day, yet they claim to follow the One Who said He is "Master of the Shabath." Yahusha's Name is nowhere to be found in their museum or publications, only the post-17th century anachronism, Jesus. This word did not exist until it appeared in the second edition of the KJV; the first edition inherited **IESV** from the Latin Vulgate.

The Hebrew Name is Yahusha, meaning *"I am your Deliverer."*

The word "revision" literally means "to look again." Reexamining the ideas we've inherited from our fathers is making YirmeYahu 16:19 very true!

"I have restrained my feet from every evil way, That I might guard Your Word. I have not turned aside from Your right-rulings, For You Yourself have taught me. How sweet to my taste has Your Word been, More than honey to my mouth!

From Your orders I get understanding; Therefore I have hated every false way. Your word is a lamp to my feet And a light to my path." – Ps. 119:101-105 It is through the Covenant that Gentiles become ingrafted to Yisharal (Eph. 2:8-13). The AIG Creation Museum could provide a room teaching the Hebrew roots of the faith, and the true Name of our Deliverer. In this same room they could provide a pool to immerse people into the true, **one Name** given among men for deliverance (Acts 4:12).

The consequences of doing this will cause AIG to become a stench in the nostrils of every Christian pastor leading his flock into damnation without the eternal Covenant, as well as all seminary professors.

The Truth will expose the Greco-Roman, man-made religion of Christianity to be:

- **a hoax**, hiding behind a Greek mask, the "New Testament language" disguising the true Name;

- **a hustle** which fused diverse Pagan customs together through "church councils",

- **a con game** that threatened and implemented mass homicides,

- **a flimflam-whopper** teaching its adherents that common bread magically **transubstantiated** into the Messiah,

- **a hood-winking swindle** promising "crusaders" a place in heaven if they killed infidels,

- **a swindling hornswoggle** that cashes-in on the ignorant, unwashed masses, and - **a bamboozling whitewash job** that rewrites history, covering its tracks of death, inquisitions, and infiltrations. Galileo Galilei was nearly burned at the stake for proving the Earth orbited the sun. The inquisitor that arrested him, Cardinal Bellarmine, has a Catholic university named after him. This kind of thing is but one example of the misplaced honor placed by the world in a system that for most of its existence believed and taught that the Earth was flat, and misled billions of people who had never brushed their teeth, showered in warm water, or flipped on a light switch. The teachers of these fantasies are recognized with titles of "doctor" and grant accreditation from the halls of learning they are spawned in. Love one another.

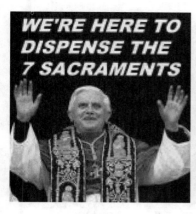

When the reapers appear, people will realize the futility of traditions. Nothing will protect (seal) us but one thing: the Name of **Yahusha** placed upon us, marking us as His property. We who have accepted His blood as the covering for our sins have been immersed in His Name. The reapers will not harm His property, but will guard us in all our ways; they will not permit us to even stub our toe (Ps. 91) in the Day of Yahuah. The Day of Yahuah will be even more fierce than the night He went through the land of Egypt slaying every first-born of men and animals whose doors did not have lamb's blood marking them.

All the first Protestants were Catholics, and remained 95% so in their practices. If you keep "Sun-day" as the Sabbath, then you are adhering to the **mark** of papal authority. **Come out of her, My people!** There are no "sacraments," so what use is there to follow the **scheme of salvation** that is offered through them?

If you do not warn them, those you might have helped with this warning will **burn just as brightly** in the lake of fire, as they would have if you had never built the Creation Museum (Ez. 18:24-26).

All **Israel** will be saved, but all those **outside** the Covenant with Yahuah will perish. Only those who are saints (qodeshim, in the Covenant) are Israel of Yahuah, His children, redeemed in Yahusha's blood. Demons **know**, and **believe** in Yahusha's atoning blood, and His resurrection. They simply will not **obey**, as Christians have been taught to **not obey**. Through Yahusha, the Gentiles are called to obedience, not called to "belief only." Even *demons* believe.

We show our belief by our outward behavior, our **obedience**.

Rom 1:5: **"Through Him and for His Name's sake, we received favor and apostleship to call people from among all the Gentiles to the obedience that comes from faith."**

If we receive a love for the Truth, it's easy to obey because we see the purpose is love. We were created to love Yahuah.

Crescent symbols originate from the worship of the host of heaven. Hinduism's symbols and practices use the zodiac to promote Nimrod's system of reincarnation, and ancestor worship.

The **sighted-moon** was adopted by the emerging Karaite sect in Babylon while captive under an Islamic Caliphate (767 CE). Recent teachers of the 20th century picked it up, and it is still echoing among newer teachers. The orthodox observe the New Moon 15 days prior to the Full Moon. When we see a crescent moon after sunset, we are looking at the fully-built first day of the moon. If you don't begin your count at zero-light, you're always one day out of phase. You can do it the best way you understand, of course, and Yahusha will correct us if we're wrong. Joining Afraim to Yahudah is more of a struggle if we continue to do things the Islamic way.

GNOSTICISM - Greek for *knowing*

A massive invasion of Nimrod's religious habits from the east occurred before, during, and after Yahusha was born. Eastern thought continues to influence the whole world as the Dali Lama is celebrated constantly. Coinciding with this invasion of enlightenment from the east, Judaism incorporated aspects of it into how they viewed themselves as above or lifted-up (exalted, *RAB*) relative to the common people.

The **RAB**, or "exalted-one" (rabbi, *my exalted-one*) emerged as a teaching authority. The Prushim (Pharisees, meaning *separated ones*) assumed the role of the **gurus**, guiding pupils into their traditions. This **nicolaitane hierarchy** (lording over the people) is hated by Yahusha for its hypocrisy. Hinduism is ancient Sun worship, and *gurus* were considered spiritual guides into enlightenment matched to the idea of rabbis. Hinduism's "4-levels" of interpretation was also brought into Judaism in what is called Kabbalism today. Many Natsarim teachers have fallen for this, and many other inherited lies. As Gnostic ideas developed, the non-physical realm was considered perfect, and the physical realm corrupt. This is why Yahukanon wrote about it at 2Yn (John) chapter 1:7:

"Because many who are leading astray went out into the world who do not confess Yahusha Mashiak as coming in the flesh. This one is he who is leading astray and the anti-mashiak."

Many Gnostic ideas were carried over from the eastern teachings of Hinduism. Another was the familiar idea of folding the hands in prayer shown in the illustration. It is called **Namaste**, and means *"the spirit in me bows to the spirit in you."* Again we perceive how the spiritual realm is regarded as perfect, and yet we are commanded to not bow to any entity but Yahuah, the Maker of all things visible and invisible.

Twisting Scripture, Bending Minds:
Commentary on Jesus.org *Question of the Day*
Re: *5 Ways Satan Wants to Destroy Your Holiness*

The author wrote: *"Legalism is not attempting to keep the law of God. It's assuming we can keep it. Furthermore, legalism says God's acceptance is found in keeping God's law. Impossible!"*
Response from Lew White:
A Christian pastor wrote that it is "impossible" to find Yahuah's acceptance by obeying Him. In Yahusha's parable at Mt. 21:28-32 about the two sons, He made the point that the one who obeys the will of the Father is acceptable. What is "impossible" is being acceptable to Yahuah by *remaining disobedient.*
In Yahusha's parable of the two sons, He shows us how our obedience DOES find acceptance: Mat 21:28-32:
"But what do you think? A man had two sons, and he came to the first and said, 'Son, go, work today in my vineyard.'
And he answering, said, 'I do not wish to,' but afterwards he repented and went.
And having come to the second, he said similarly.
And he answering, said, 'I go, master,' but he did not go.
Which of the two did the desire of the father?" They said to Him, "The first." Yahusha said to them, "Truly, I say to you that tax collectors and whores are entering into the reign of Alahim before you, for Yahukanon came to you in the way of righteousness, and you did not believe him, but tax collectors and whores believed him. And when you saw it, you did not repent afterwards, to believe him."

Our obedience *perfects* and establishes our belief. New laws invented by men (like Sunday) have replaced the Torah of Yahuah.

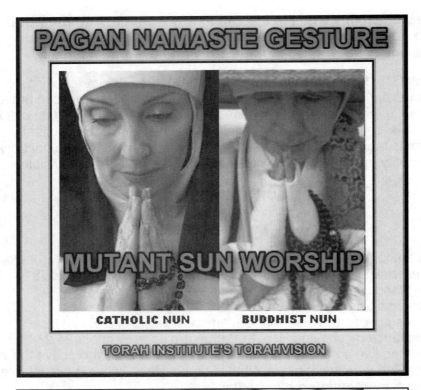

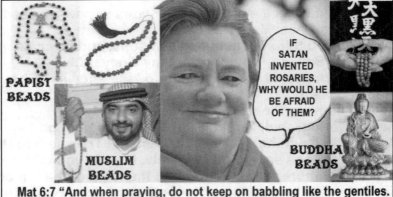

Mat 6:7 "And when praying, do not keep on babbling like the gentiles. For they think that they shall be heard for their many words."

In the 2ⁿᵈ century BCE, Egyptian worshippers of Serapis were called by the Greek term: *Christians*.

They bowed to crux-shaped objects, the ancient symbol of the Sun. The roots of Christianity originate from Greek Suncults in Egypt, but Constantine formally adopted all the pagan Sun worship together with the Roman Suncult's existing Magisterium. The Roman Kaiser/pope and cardinals' overt Sun worship became veiled, yet remained intact.

Babel's mother of harlots wore the disguise of Christianity as the 4th beast, but today the Natsarim are pulling up her skirt for all to see.
A great deal of Babel's Sun worship came through Hinduism, even the "holy waters" of the Ganges was brought over into early Catholicism. The halos on statues are seen first in Hinduism's idolatry, and also adopted by early Catholicism.
The prayer beads (repetitive prayers) came into Catholicism later, adopted from Hinduism through Islam at Fatima, a city in Spain captured from the Moors by Catholics. An apparition of "Mary" handed the beads to several children, and off they went with more arrogant nonsense. The reapers will remove all things offensive, so we have to learn to do the things that are pleasing to Him.

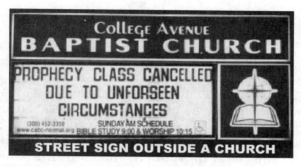

STREET SIGN OUTSIDE A CHURCH

Don't follow any teaching authority but one: Yahusha.

THE MAGISTERIUM
The Great Babel Head - Nimrod

Since the beginning of civilization and the first king on Earth, a struggle to control the minds (hearts) of all mankind has never ceased.
The first king was Nimrod, the mighty hunter of men.

Babel's authority to reign is empowered by the dragon.

After Nimrod's death the population revered him by worshipping the Sun. Looking down from "heaven," he was believed to be the "Great Architect." People worshipped the host of heaven - the creation - rather than the Creator. Since Babel is the head of the beast authority, we could call Nimrod the Great Babel Head.

THE NATIONS WENT MAD

There's a source, or wellspring from which all the Earth has become drunk. It is personified to be a **woman** who causes all the world to be drunk on the contents of a "golden cup." Revelation calls her the mother of harlots or Babel the Great. YirmeYahu (Jer.) 7 & 44 refer to her as the **"queen of heaven."** Jer/YirmeYahu 51:7: **"Babel was a golden cup in the hand of Yahuah, making drunk all the Earth. The nations drank her wine, that is why the nations went mad!"**
The Great Mother rides the beast.

WHAT IS THE BEAST?

The beast is not a person, but a teaching authority promoting all the fertility practices everyone is blind to, though they are in plain sight of everyone.

The beast is the **reign of Babel**, the teaching authority that will end at the coming of Yahusha's reign. This is why at His coming **the reign** becomes the **reign of Yahusha**. Note Rev. 11:15:

"And the 7th messenger sounded, and there came to be loud voices in the heaven, saying, 'The **reign** of this world has become *the reign* of our Master, and of His Messiah, and He shall reign forever and ever!'"

BABEL'S REIGN FALLS

"And he cried with a mighty voice, saying, 'Babel the great is fallen, is fallen, and has become a dwelling place of demons, a haunt for every unclean spirit, and a haunt for every unclean and hated bird, because all the nations have drunk of the wine of the wrath of her whoring, and the sovereigns of the earth have committed whoring with her, and the merchants of the earth have become rich through the power of her riotous living.' And I heard another voice from the heaven saying, **'Come out of her, my people, lest you share in her sins, and lest**

you receive of her plagues." - Rev 18:2-4

Birthday celebrations originate from Babel's worship of the host of heaven. They are the foundation of Astrology, and such celebrating is witchcraft. It's the oldest form of idolatry and found in every culture on Earth. All sorcery flows from Babel, and Yahuah shows us how to guard against it, and show love for Him: **"You do not make for yourself a carved image, or any likeness of that which is in the shamayim above, or which is in the arets beneath, or which is in the mayim under the arets, you do not bow down to them nor serve them. For I, Yahuah your Alahim, am a jealous Al, visiting the crookedness of the fathers on the children to the 3rd and 4th generations of those who hate Me, but showing kindness to thousands, to those who love Me and guard My commands."** Ex 20

At Yekezqal (Ezekiel) 8:10, **animals** (zoo, zodiac) are seen on the inner walls of Yahuah's Temple. Before they killed him, Stephen told the Sanhedrin about their worshipping the host of heaven: *"So Alahim turned and gave them up to worship the **host of the heaven."*** - Act 7:42

NIMROD - ORION - SAGITTARIUS
BABEL'S OLD RELIGION
ZODIAC - HOROSCOPE - ASTROLOGY

Nimrod Sun deities: often shown holding hunting equipment

ZODIAC MAZZAROTH - The Source Of All Sorcery

The word mazzaroth refers to the host of heaven; a collective term for the sun, moon, planets, quasars, stars, comets, nebulae, and galaxies. The harlot woman, Babel the great, is an idiomatic term for the *teachings* of Babel. It (she) teaches the false worship of the host of heaven, through which all the nations have been deceived. Stephen spoke of it to the Sanhedrin. Rev. 2 refers to it as the **teachings of Izebel.** It is a stronghold that has crept into the hearts of some Natsarim teachers, and is capable of deceiving the elect (chosen ones). Babel's occult (hidden) behavior offends Yahuah. Worshipping (or fearing) the omens of animal shapes thought to be living in the sky, mankind has a long record of idolatry inherited from the astral woman of Revelation 17, Babel.

Her *teachings* have infected the whole world. Sometimes we hear this woman referred to as "Mother Nature" in the secular media. False behavior and beliefs have been embraced, even by some modern Natsarim.

Some teach that the **secret mystery of deliverance** has been *"written in the stars,"* an idea first published in a 19th-century novel *Mazzaroth* by Francis Rolleston. Alexander Hislop's *Two Babylons* was written to counter some of the false claims made in the book *Mazzaroth*.

The Catholic cardinal John Henry Newman had to respond to Hislop with his own book, *An Essay On The Development of Christian Doctrine.* The theologian Ethelbert William Bullinger believed the false information in *Mazzaroth*, and wrote his own book, *Witness of The Stars.* It shows from Scripture how Yahuah feels about the nations worshipping the host of heaven. Any mixing or **syncretism** (especially the zodiac) arouses His most fierce wrath.

People overlook how Stephen confronted the Sanhedrin with their fascination with the **host of heaven.** We have to stay alert to any false teachings using the constellations to predict the return of Yahusha, or His work of redemption. Syncretism is the mixture of differing beliefs. **The dragon invented the zodiac, but Yahuah made the stars.** The message **of deliverance** is not found in the stars, but rather it is found in the prophetic Word of Yahuah. Peter describes the defilements of this deluded kosmic system at 2Pet 2:18-22. We must not return to the corruption as a dog returns to its vomit. The old religion of Babel lures through the enticement of sexual love, and is a scheme of the devil. Compatibility is not directed through horoscopes or magical spells.

There are Christian and Natsarim teachers claiming the "gospel" or message is written in the constellations. Yahusha's **redemption plan** is not recorded in stars, but rather in the Scriptures as shadows through the 7 festivals (appointed times): **Pesach, Matsah, Bikkurim, Shabuoth, Yom Teruah, Yom Kafar, and Sukkoth.**

Yekezqal (Ezekiel) chapter 8 records that Yahuah's people had forsaken Him by placing these symbols inside His Dwelling Place: **"And I went in and looked and saw all kinds of creeping creatures, abominable beasts, and all the idols of the house of Yisharal, carved all around on the walls."** Ez 8:10 Many synagogues were decorated with **zodiacs** on walls and floors.

The signs of the **Zodiac** are a living **ZOO** of imaginary creatures depicted in the heavens by connecting the dots of stars. Yahuah created the lights to be for signs and seasons. These "signs" are **signals**, not **messages** within themselves. The "signs" signal the appointments which reveal the **redemption plan.** The shadows of things to come are the 7 appointed times (moedim). It is a crafty scheme to shift our attention away from the true shadows of redemption and teach Babel's zodiac signs instead. Yahuah specifically commanded us to **not** fear the signs of the heavens in the way of the gentiles: **"Thus said Yahuah, 'Do not learn the way of the gentiles, and do not be awed by the signs of the heavens, for the gentiles are awed by them."** – Jer/YirmeYahu 10:2 Making Scripture say things it doesn't say is to *feed on wormwood*. **"The heavens are proclaiming the esteem of Al; And the expanse is declaring the work of His hand. Day to day pours forth speech, And night to night reveals knowledge."** - Ps. 19:1-2

Has Yahuah ever told us to connect the stars into the shapes of animals? E. W. Bullinger's book, *Witness of the Stars* uses Psalm 19 as a basis, and uses Astrology to confirm Yahuah's Word. The man was brilliant, but he embraced Babel's zodiac. It was the only knowledge of the skies available to him at the time. Since his time, our understanding has vastly increased.

People have **turned aside to myths**, as Paul warned us at 2Tim 4. Babel's mythological patterns draw us away from true worship. Yahuah tells us: "**. . . and lest you lift up your eyes to the heavens, and shall see the sun, and the moon, and the stars all the host of the heavens – and you be drawn away into bowing down to them and serving them, which Yahuah your Alahim has allotted to all the peoples under all the heavens.**" – Dt. 4:19

The message of redemption is not found in the shapes and designs imagined to be in the skies, but it's found in the inspired Word of Yahuah.

What's your **sign**? Is it resting on Shabath, or a constellation?

The festivals of Yahuah are shadows (outlines) of Yisharal's redemption. Babel never had the plan, and never will. We are told to come out of her, not invent imaginary meanings about the shapes of animals thought to live in the skies. Astrology is Babel's false path to love. Yahuah's **Commandments** *teach us how to love.*

Psalm 19 is often quoted by those promoting the zodiac as showing us the **redemption plan**. This is a lie.

This same Psalm speaks of the Torah of Yahuah being clean, perfect, and more desirable than fine gold. Yahuah's Torah doesn't teach us the zodiac, but warns us against it.

Yahuah shares His heart with us by leading us in His Word.

"And I shall give you shepherds according to My heart, and they shall feed you with knowledge and understanding." - YirmeYahu 3:15

"Let the words of my mouth and the meditation of my heart be pleasing before You, O Yahuah, my Rock and my Redeemer."
- Psa 19:14

Nimrod's influences are striving to control the world so the dragon is obeyed. Being aware of the scheme is the first step, then we have to decide not to participate in the witchcraft.

THE MAGISTERIUM CONTROLS BELIEFS

Babel's controlling authority over what people believe and practice evolved into the totalitarian magisterium the world calls the Roman Catholic Church. It has always been here since the founding of Babel, but has gone by many other names.

The most recent form of this beastly world government grew from its Roman roots, which openly worshipped the Sun deity Apollo Sol Invictus. Constantine merged, or synthesized, diverse Sun worshipping bodies together into a universal pattern of behavior. Mithraism, Zoroastrianism, Hinduism, and Manichaean customs were blended into a new mold, and these pagan forms of witchcraft came together into a new shape. Sun worship has shape-shifted, and can still be found where there are pillars, crosses (solar symbol), and meetings in the morning on the Day of the Sun, Sunday.

(See Sunday Origins Book on Facebook, Amazon, and at www.torahzone.net) This beastly World Order channels Babel's power in three divisions: Clergy-Nobility-Laity. It has been so since the days of Nimrod, the Great Architect of the World Order. This magisterium is Babel going under another name, and all the reigns of the Earth are controlled as surely as a beast is controlled by a ring in its nose. Babel's world government poses as a religious institution. Over the centuries it has set up a list of "dogmas" and requires its adherents to accept them with absolute devotion. This beast behaves like a chameleon, adopting the practices and symbols of indigenous populations and changing their meaning. Behind all the symbols and practices is the ancient religion of Babel: Sun worship, and the worship of the "host of heaven."

This organization considers itself the only path to salvation through its dogmas. Salvation is understood to be solely through the dispensation of seven sacraments, available exclusively through the priesthood of the "one true mother church." Failure to believe in any one dogma is grounds for excommunication. For many centuries those who resisted the authority of this mother church were burned at the stake as heretics.

This magisterium is the source of such doctrines as **Purgatory, eternal suffering in fire, relic kissing** (veneration of human remains)**, transubstantiation** (bread wafer transforms into living body and blood of Yahusha with words "hoc est corpus meum")**, statue veneration** (kneeling before objects)**, steeples/sun pillars, bells, worship of the "host"** (in a monstrance – sun burst object)**, prayers to the dead** (necromancy via rosaries)**, monks, nuns, popes, priests, celibacy, indulgences, trinity doctrine, infant baptism, apostolic succession, sacraments, crosses** (symbol of Sun deity everywhere throughout history)**, replacement of Name Yahuah to "LORD"** (Baal)**, adoption of Easter / Ishtar fertility festival with sunrise worship & egg/bunny/fish symbols, Natalis Sol Invictus** (Saturnalia) **transformed into "Christ-Mass," a celebration of Yahusha's birth**, - and much more. They are generally doing everything Yahuah ordered not to be done, while ignoring everything He told us to guard and observe. They forbade the Scriptures from the "laity." Laity means "the people," the bottom level of their **World Order** of clergy-nobility-laity, or 3 *estates*.

This magisterium is the source from which Protestants have inherited many of their doctrines and behavior. The belief in *"one god in three persons"* **defines** Catholicism according to Athanasius, one of the attendees of the Nicene Council in 325. Athanasius was from

Alexandria's Didascalia (teaching authority), and is dubbed the *"father of orthodoxy."* Ortho-doxy literally means *"upright teaching."*
Natsarim throughout history were considered heretics by this teaching authority, and were held to be *anathema* (worthy of death).
Natsarim work to teach the Truth, and reject the teaching authority of the magisterium, and all those following its rebellious practices.
Everything in the list above is witchcraft, carefully fed to the masses over many centuries. Abiding in Yahuah's Word sets us free from false beliefs.

The tendency for us to make judgments about what others believe became a **totalitarian magisterium** the world calls the Roman Catholic Church. This beastly World Order is an **authoritarian world government** posing as a religious institution. It has set up a list of dogmas requiring its adherents to accept with absolute devotion.
This organization considers itself the only path to salvation through its dogmas.
To not believe in one dogma is grounds for excommunication, and in past centuries this meant death, often by burning at the stake. They were not kidding around about their authority over the whole world.
The Protestant Reformation caused the nobility to turn away from the head of this government, wounding it severely to death. The response to this wounding to the head came immediately through a Spanish soldier named Ignatius de Loyola.
He founded a new society to fight against those opposed to the papacy at Montmartre, France, August 15, 1534.
It was officially recognized by a Papal Bull in 1540.
It is a counter-Reformation which Loyola referred to as **Regimini Militantis Ecclesiae**, Latin for *"to the government of the church militant."*
The objective of the Societas IESU, or Jesuits, is to restore the authority of the papacy over the world.

TRANSUBSTANTIATION

TRANSUBSTANTIATION - A Catholic Doctrine

The doctrine of transubstantiation was adopted in the year 1215, and caused many who did not believe it to be burned at the stake by the Inquisitors. It's believed that when an ordained priest utters the Latin words "hoc est corpus meum" (this is my body), a bit of bread and wine miraculously transforms from bread into the living body and blood of Yahusha.

In other words, they are performing a miracle, yet as often as they may do so, such miracles somehow don't count in declaring the priest a "saint."

They believe the substance has changed, but only *appears* to still be bread and wine. How about if they said they'd changed lead into gold, but it still appeared to be lead? Imagine a bowling ball someone claims changed into a golf ball, yet remained in appearance as a bowling ball. Millions of intelligent adults faithfully believe the doctrine of transubstantiation.

If this *sacrament* is a false teaching, so are all the others.

TRANSUBSTANTIATING
LEAD INTO GOLD
WASN'T WORKING
SO THEY TRIED SOMETHING DIFFERENT

BY WHAT AUTHORITY DO YOU DO THESE THINGS?

Yahusha's teaching authority was questioned by the chief priests and elders at Mt. 21:23. **They had set up their own authority.**
I went online to *AskACatholic* and posted this question:

"Yahusha's teaching authority was questioned by the chief priests and elders at Mt. 21:23. To them, Yahusha was a heretic not following their authority to teach (they had not ordained Him!). They, like the existing Magisterium, had set up their own authority, above Scripture. They added and took away whatever they liked. What is the name of the one you worship? And, if you claim it is Yahuah, what example of obedience to Him can you offer as a sign of that worship?

As Christianity evolved over many centuries, many alterations occurred such that resting from work on the Sabbath became transferred to the first day, and abstaining from unclean animals was no longer required.

As there are no examples given from Scripture of these and many other practices now adopted, it has been said that "church tradition" retains authority to do the very same things that enraged Yahusha's wrath about the Sanhedrin in His day.

In this context, praying to dead people (necromancy and divination) would seem to be another example of such church tradition. If Yahuah does not change, and such things are an abomination to Him, by what authority do you do these things, and by what name do you call on for deliverance?"

IS THE MAGISTERIUM INFALLIBLE?

The Scriptures are interpreted by the living Spirit of Yahusha in a believer, guiding us into all Truth, not by a hierarchy imposing its authority over us. Yahusha is our only teaching authority, and we are all brothers and sisters. Nicolaitane behavior is hated by Yahusha. The doctrine of "apostolic succession" is a man-made tradition. Because the Natsarim have always ignored the authority of the Roman Circus, we were forced to hide in the valleys (Waldensians). The Alexandrian Cult wrote about us, condemning us for living according to the Torah, seeing no difference between us and the Yahudim, except that we believe in Yahusha. If the Roman Circus is infallible, how did they manage to alter the 4th Commandment, the sign of the eternal Covenant, to the Day of the Sun? Yahuah told us not to erect a pillar anywhere (Lev / Uyiqra 26:1), so the Circus puts them on every building they can find. The infallible aspect seems to pertain to the ability to never miss a chance to disobey. What Yahuah told us to never do, they do. What He told us to do, they avoid like the plague. The reason the reapers are about to be released is because men have broken the everlasting Covenant: "See, Yahuah is making the earth empty and making it waste, and shall overturn its surface, and shall scatter abroad its inhabitants. And it shall be – as with the people so with the priest, as with the servant so with his master, as with the female servant so with her mistress, as with the buyer so with the seller, as with the lender so with the borrower, as with the creditor so with the debtor; the earth is completely emptied and utterly plundered, for Yahuah has spoken this word.

The Earth shall mourn and wither, the world shall languish and wither, the haughty people of the earth shall languish. For the earth has been defiled under its inhabitants, because they have transgressed the Toroth, changed the law, broken the everlasting Covenant." (YashaYahu / Is. 24:1-5). You can't fix this with holy water, sacraments, and powerless prayers to someone named Jesus, because that's not His Name, and it never will be. His Name is Yahusha, and means *"I am your Deliverer."* Partially translated, it can also mean *"Yah is our Deliverer."* He is Yahuah incarnate. There is no Trinity, or Yahuah would have told us He is three, not one.

Praying to dead people (necromancy) only makes Him more furious, and to teach people to do so is beyond belief. Sorry, but I had to tell you these things. We must not continue in arrogant nonsense; we must repent and obey the witness of Yahusha. He faced the same kind of human resistance in His own people; a hierarchy that did not obey Him set themselves up over the people. The Magisterium is the current head of the beast, given Babel's Sun worshipping teaching authority by the dragon.

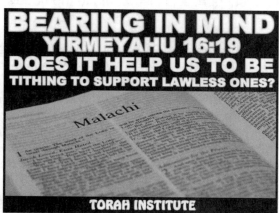

HOW ARE WE TO TITHE?

Everyone would agree there is a great deal of theological confusion. Yahuah does not change in any way; there is no shadow of turning. And yet, time, circumstances, and altered teachings make it seem that what He once called an abomination is now pleasing to Him. How so? Men teach us the 7th day of rest is outlawed (by order of the Catholic Council of Laodicea, 363-364 CE, canon 29), that we may eat unclean animals for food, and that most of Yahuah's Commandments are now annulled, having been "nailed to the crux."

They didn't nail "tithing" to the crux, but kept it in force.

Why do Christian pastors teach against obedience to the Ten Commandments, yet complain when people don't tithe? If keeping the Ten Commandments is being "legalistic," then how could tithing (to those telling you to do so) not be the same?

The Truth is, we are to obey in every way, and being legal in Yahusha's eyes is very, very good; we should pursue living exactly as He lived. Tithing is an arrangement established on the principle of giving back to Yahuah.

Ten percent of our increase is the base amount that everyone is to render, and it is fair because it is the same for everyone, as a flat tax would be. It is more blessed to give than to receive for many reasons, and expresses to Yahuah that we recognize how He is worthy of a portion of our labor.

We have nothing at all that we have not received (1Cor. 4:7). Abraham gave a tenth of the booty to the priest of Salem, indicating it may be more than only food, although the most common tithe involved the giving of animals and produce during the festival times.

While the Temple stood, prior to 70 CE, the tithe was given to the priesthood for their support, and distributed to the needy of the assembly.

With the destruction of the Temple and its operation, this priesthood has been suspended, and in the Renewed Covenant we are under our High Priest of the order of Malkizedeq. We are Yahusha's followers if we are immersed and under His authority. His function in this priesthood is primarily one of *announcing the coming of His reign,* and *repenting to be restored to favor* (2Cor. 5:18-20, Col. 1:21).

We teach the nations everything He commanded us to obey, and live by every Word that proceeds from the mouth of Yahuah.

As His ambassadors, we continue to function in His power, and we still give to those in need of support.

We are obliged to note any needs in our own family in order that they not be a burden on the assembly.

Teachers have always been all over the map in regard to how to tithe properly, but Yahusha is our Teacher on this subject.

Teachers must not focus the tithe on themselves receiving it, only to partake in it to sustain them as they work in the harvest.

His Word is trustworthy, but the words of men are not. Here are some texts to whet your appetite on discerning His will about the tithe:

"If any believing man or woman has widows, let such assist them, and do not let the assembly be burdened, in order to assist those who are truly widows. Let the elders who rule well be counted

worthy of double respect, especially those who labor in the word and teaching. For the Scripture says, 'You shall not muzzle an ox while it treads out the grain,' and, 'The laborer is worthy of his wages.'" - 1 Timothy 5:16-18 - See also: 1 Thessalonians chapter 5, Acts 4, 1 Yn. 3:17, and 1 Timothy chapter 5

SCRIPTURE TWISTING HAPPENS

"LET US MAKE MAN IN OUR IMAGE"

This twist was made long ago by a single translator, then repeated by subsequent translators.

The verse mostly referred to by Trinitarians is Barashith / Genesis 1:26, and it is not discussing the make-up of *Yahuah*, but rather **Adam**.

In a similar way, teachers misunderstand the context of **"Who do men say the Son of Adam is?"** (Mt. 16).

The discussion is not about *who Peter is*, but *Who Yahusha is*.

The mistranslation of Genesis 1:26 causes a disconnection from Genesis 2:7. Traditionalists will be very disturbed about this.

Bereshith / Genesis 1:26 is often cited to prove the Creator (Yahuah) is more than one, in spite of the *"Shema"* at Dt. 6:4.

Yahusha acknowledged it was the "greatest" of all Torah instructions:

"Hear (SHEMA) Yisharal, Yahuah our Alahim, Yahuah is ONE."

The Hebrew words abstractly apply to ruling with the *character traits* of the Creator, rather than the *appearance* of the first man.

This verse at Genesis 1:26 is a classic example of how each translation follows the errors of the previous ones, very much like lemmings following one another over a cliff.

As we analyze the Hebrew words, we encounter things that don't match the meaning we've inherited. The translators, either by ignorance or intentional misdirection, altered the whole sentence.

There is no **"Let Us make,"** nor an **"Our image"** in the Hebrew. This twisting of Scripture was made long ago by a single translator, and then repeated by subsequent translators.

The sentence in the Hebrew at Bereshith 1:26 is recording the executive decision of Yahuah to *"breathe into"* the **Adam** (humanity) His *"essence."* As Yahuah was doing all this He was speaking with

77

His other creatures, the malakim (angelic beings), expressing His plan. We know who He is speaking to from the book of Jubilees [Yubal], and they were singing as He did so [Ayub / Job 38:7].

His Own **breath of life** would instill His character traits, discernment, and emotional capacity from the "wind," or RUACH, placing a living NEFESH into the Adam.

The Hebrew words NEFESH, NEKASH, and NESHAH refer to "breath" or "breathing," not "making."

Let's look very closely at the actual Hebrew words:

The first 7 words of the sentence at Bereshith 1:26: [NOTE: the "**NU**" refers to **shared** or **same** in this context, rather than **our**]

U'YAMAR – ALAHIM - **NESHAH** –   ADAM – B'**TSELEM'NU** – KADEMUTH'**NU** - U'YARADU

and He said – Alahim – I breathe into – Adam – in same essence – same character – that they rule

The words above are the first 7 Hebrew words that are better interpreted in the context of Yahuah's plan for Adam to **"rule"** with His **character**:

1:26 "And Alahim said, " (I) Breathe into [NESHAH] Adam [humanity] a shared **essence**, with a shared **character**, and **let them rule** over the fish of the sea, and over the birds of the shamayim, and over the livestock, and over all the arets and over all the creeping creatures that creep on the arets." 1:27 And Alahim [alef-tau] created the man in His essence, in the essence of Alahim He created him; male and female He created them." - **BYNV**

   The word **TSELEM** is the 5th word, and when taken *literally* it means an *image*, as a form, or shape.

TSELEM in the abstract means **"essence,"** a reflection of the traits, judgments, emotional capacity, intellect, and so on. Certainly our physical form is not what this sentence is expressing at all.

The former translators forced the Hebrew word "NESHAH" to mean *"Let Us make."*

There is no "let," "Us," or "make" in the word NESHAH.

   NESHAH is cognate with the Hebrew word NAKASH, *"to breathe,"* and NEFESH, a living being.

It's important to keep breathing, or your "breath" [NEFESH] will return to the One that gave it.

Notice Yahuah reflects on what He has done at Bereshith 2:7, He *"breathed" into* the man He had formed out of dust:

2:7: **"And Yahuah Alahim formed the man out of dust from the ground, and breathed into his nostrils breath of life. And the man became a living being." - BYNV**

   The objective is for Adam to "rule" like Yahuah, not "look" like Yahuah. The "**NU**" can mean "us," but in this context it expresses the idea of something shared or being shared. The Hebrew word ABINU can be expressed **"our** father." What is being shared is the father, so the expression **"NU"** is expressing that Yahuah's "essence" is being shared with Adam.

When Hebrew is expressing an abstract meaning, the conditioning from the literal can block comprehension.

There is a direct connection between Gen. 1:26 and 2:7. The Adam was created / formed, then Yahuah breathed (NEFAQ, puffed) into his nostrils the breath (NESHAMAH, wind) of kayim (life). This connection between 1:26 & 2:7 is difficult using the inherited translations, but when corrected we immediately see the "breathing" involved. Gen. 2:7 is sequentially AFTER the seventh day, but what it describes happened on the 6th day. It is only a recap of what Yahuah did, not another creative act. Knowledge is increasing, it didn't stop at the KJV. The argument ends when we correctly translate the meaning of the inspired words. There is no *"Let Us make"* in the sentence at all. There is no *"Our image"* in the sentence.

It is a Trinitarian interpretation of the text, nothing more. Once you've seen it, you can connect the idea at **1:26** to **2:7**. Or, you can ignore this entirely, and go back to thinking what you used to about the sentence. I still love you.

DEMONOLOGY

What we call "demons" are very powerful spiritual beings. The war in the heavenlies is going on constantly, even while we sleep. Our fear is not to be the one who can kill the body only. One of Yahuah's messengers slew 185,000 Assyrians in one night, and didn't wake the others with them. (see Is / YashaYahu 37:36) We have no idea how powerful they actually are, but if we are immersed in the Name of Yahusha, we are sealed for the day of redemption, and the messengers protect us so we will not even stub our toe: **"No evil befalls you, And a plague does not come near your tent; For He commands His messengers concerning you, To guard you in all your ways. They bear you up in their hands, Lest you dash your foot against a stone.** (stub your toe) **You tread upon lion and cobra, Young lion and serpent you trample under foot. Because he cleaves to Me in love, Therefore I deliver him; I set him on high, Because he has known My Name. When he calls on Me, I answer him; I am with him in distress; I deliver him and esteem him. With long life I satisfy him, And show him My deliverance."** -Ps 91:11-16

As We Wait For Eternity To Arrive

The perspective of eternity is in our hearts because we share Yahusha's Mind, but eternity is not in the hearts of those living in the mind of the flesh. Yahuah can form a diamond or precious metal with the same ease as forming iron or sand. He cannot be bribed with anything, since He is the Possessor of heaven and earth already. He's the Owner, we're only tenants. We see things His way way if we belong to Him, and our most precious treasure is to know Him.
We were created to be His companions, and Yahusha gave us this insight at Yahukanon (John) 15. We have to be careful not to judge others, since only Yahusha knows what is in their heart.
"Do not slander a servant to his master, Lest he curse you, And you be found guilty." Proverbs 30:10
Our motivation is to serve Him, and His body; all else ranks below these. We give preference to all others, not to ourselves.
Romans 12 and Ephesians 4 need to be read often to remind us of who we are in relation toward one another in Yahuah's sight.
"In brotherly love, tenderly loving towards one another, in appreciation, giving preference to each other . . ." - Romans 12:10
Our consideration for others' hearts – our tenderhearted attitude – is one of the most important behavioral differences between us and those of the world.
As long as we abide in Yahusha's will for all His body, He will guide, build-up, and equip us for every good work.

RESTORING A PURE LIP: HEBREW

Our understanding of Scripture is enhanced when we learn more about the original language it was inspired in, spoken by our Deliverer.
The Hebrew script is mistakenly called *"Phoenician"* in many resources, and the Aramaic is mistakenly called "modern Hebrew." No wonder it's a struggle to learn true Hebrew. Now there are people combining Hieroglyphics with sprinklings of Hebrew on the Internet, claiming the original Hebrew script originated from the Hyksos, who

were illiterate slaves working in turquoise mines for Egyptians in the Sinai Peninsula.

The third letter in the Name of Yahuah (yod-hay-UAU-hay) is the original sound of our letter "U." We hear it in the phrase hallelU-Yah, and it can be heard in the name of the tribe YAHUDAH (yod-hay-UAU-daleth-hay). This letter became the Greek letter UPSILON, and even retained the same original shape from the Hebrew script like (Y). Scholars mistakenly refer to the true Hebrew script as "Phoenician," and they refer to the Aramaic script as "modern Hebrew." Later, the Masoretes stepped in to corrupt the vowels for 500 years (700's through 1100's), inventing their own system to befoul the utterance of the Name. People are so confused today they are teaching innocent hearts that there are "no written vowels in the Hebrew language." Ridiculous - The Hebrew letters ALEF, AYIN, UAU, YOD, and HAY are written vowels. Clement of Alexandria wrote the Name YAHUAH using the Greek vowels inherited from the Hebrew: IAOUE. The Latin vowels came from the Greek, the Greek vowels came from the Hebrew. There's no "double-U" in any of these. Our modern letter "W" was an invention by a typesetter who combined two Latin letters UU, but shaped VV, becoming the "double-U' letter we now use today.

The Latin V is a U, not our modern V. It is shaped V because the Greek UPSILON (shaped Y) lost the lower stem passing into Latin. The original Hebrew letter UAU is shaped **Y** - but to see it you have to understand that scholars mistakenly call this letter *Phoenician*, which itself is a Greek word **invented** by Herodotus in the 5th century BCE. How do we pronounce the Name using the four vowels YOD-HAY-UAU-HAY? We have to study the original Hebrew alphabet (Alef-Beth). Someone asked, "is there is a sound of "W" in any Hebrew words?" This is a simple question, and yet it has to be answered without guile. The sounding of words (transliterating) can take on a variety of foreign letters phonetically. This is known as phonology, the way words sound. We might write a foreign word with our letters, but the objective is to achieve the same sound. The word "right" and the word "write" sound the same, and are known as "homonyms." One could argue how we hear our modern letter "W" in a Hebrew word, however we must consider that we can easily pass errors into the future by using letters phonetically that may confuse future generations. There is no letter "J" in Hebrew, neither is there a "W." Encyclopedias contain technical errors which teachers like ourselves may not detect easily, but when we do, we are responsible to pass the Truth forward.

WHY WE BABBLE THE NAME OF THE CREATOR

There's a Commandment pertaining to the Name, yet the whole world is babbling it. It began long ago as a result of Nimrod's building project. Our tongues, (lips, languages) became confused by Yahuah because of rebellion.

We often hear these kinds of comments: *"I don't speak Hebrew!"*
"He knows who I mean or I can call Him whatever I want!"
They have an unwillingness to be healed, because they don't even know they are sick.

We have LIGHT, but what we need now is EYESIGHT to cure the blindness.

"I have decided to assemble the nations, to gather the kingdoms and to pour out my wrath on them- all my fierce anger. The whole world will be consumed by the fire of my jealous anger.
Then will I purify the lips of the peoples, that all of them
may call on the Name of Yahuah and serve Him shoulder to shoulder." – ZefanYah 3:8-9

"Adam lay with his wife again, and she gave birth to a son and named him Seth, saying, 'Alahim has granted me another child in place of Abel, since Kain killed him.' Seth also had a son, and he named him Anosh. At that time men began to call on the Name of YAHUAH." Gen/Barashith 4:25-26

"Who has ascended up into heaven, or descended? Who has gathered the wind in His fists? Who has bound the waters in a garment? Who has established all the ends of the Earth?
What is His Name, and what is His Son's Name, if you can tell?" - Prov 30:4

This refers directly to the 3rd Commandment, where the Name of Yahuah is to be honorable and never brought to naught, expunged, laid waste, or ruined.

"You do not take the Name of YAHUAH your Alahim in vain; for YAHUAH will not hold him guiltless that takes His Name in vain." – Exodus/Shemoth 20:7

A dictionary definition for vain: *"ineffectual or unsuccessful; futile; a VAIN effort; without significance, value, or importance; baseless or worthless."*

The inspired Hebrew word which we translate the word VAIN from is shin-uau-alef, SHOAH, #7724 and this is the definition of it in Hebrew: Devastation, ruin, perish, lay waste; DESTROY.

To destroy, omit, miss, obfuscate, circumlocute, substitute, shun, ignore, deny, change, ruin, or treat lightly is the meaning of SHOAH. *YOM HA SHOAH* is a modern-day remembrance of the Holocaust, when 6 million Yahudim perished.

YAHUAH: Yod Hay Uau Hay (four vowels)
The letter W is a new letter. The French resisted adopting a foreign letter, so they wrote it as "VV," and called it "double-vay."

YAHUDAH: Yod Hay Uau Daleth Hay
6th Hebrew letter UAU: "oo" or "o"
Our modern letter "double-U" is new letter (UU). The ancient Hebrew form letter sounds like our U. Later it became the Greek Upsilon shaped "Y" - also equivalent to our modern letter U. We hear the *"OO"* sound of the sixth letter (as in the word school) in the following Hebrew phrase: **Hallelu Yah**, as well as the names **Yahudah** and **Lui**.

Yahusha is the Mediator of all Covenants with Yisharal, and He writes a love for the Torah upon our hearts. His circumcision of our heart is the "Renewed Covenant" and it is with the "house of Yisharal" and the "house of Yahudah" (YirmeYahu/Jer 31, Heb. 8). Christians that hear the word "Yisharal" often mistake the word "Jewish" (one of the tribes, Yahudah) and confuse us with "Rabbinical Judaism." Yahusha is our only teaching authority, not any man-made ruling committee or religious group.

HOW TO DISTINQUISH NAMES FROM TITLES
James Brown – a name, the exclusive personal noun, his "contract name." The title, *Godfather of Soul,* informs what the person is about, his "renown," or what he's *known* for. Michael Jackson is "known" as the *King of Pop*. There is no reference to "Names" (plural) for Yahuah. He has only <u>one</u> Name.

A name is a personal, specific designation. When Yahuah's Name is used in Scripture, it refers exclusively to one word used at least 6,823 times: "YAHUAH." This Name is the personal, proper name by which Yahuah is known, and in this Name alone He makes each of His Covenants. It is identical to a "brand" or "trademark." A "pronoun" can be used to identify a function or role, such as "father." A personal pronoun identifies a specific person. A "name" is exclusive identification.

A boat is a thing. If we name the boat, we specify one boat from all the other boats. The term "GOD" is a prime example of this idea. Without naming the specific being we intend to specify, a listener can fill-in whatever being they may be thinking of. Tradition has caused us to inherit GENERIC names, causing the masses to vainly call on the true Creator. If we use generic terms like god, Christ, or lord, we are employing general, non-specific, and non-exclusive words to describe what we intend to say.

Isa/YashaYahu 42:8 states:

"I am Yahuah, that is My Name, and My esteem I do not give to another, nor My praise to idols."

Prov 18:10: **"The Name of Yahuah is a strong tower; the righteous run to it and are safe."**

IS YAHUSHA YAHUAH?

Let's look at what He says about it.

YashaYahu 43:11 states:

"I, I am Yahuah, and besides Me there is no Deliverer."

The meaning of many Hebrew words clarify Who Yahuah is:

YAHUAH: I WAS, I AM, I WILL BE
YAHUAH ALAHIM: I AM YOUR LOFTY ONE
YAHUAH RAFA: I AM YOUR HEALER
YAHUAH YIREH: I AM YOUR PROVIDER
YAHUAH ADONAI: I AM YOUR SOVEREIGN
YAHUAH AL SHADDAI: I AM MIGHTY OVERWHELMINGLY
YAHUAH SHALOM: I AM COMPLETENESS (PEACEFULNESS)
YAHUAH RO: I AM YOUR SHEPHERD
YAHUSHA: I AM YOUR DELIVERER

His identity has been hidden in countless controversial disputes, and it cannot be known unless it is revealed to you by Him:

Luke 10:22-24: **"'All has been delivered to Me by My Father, and no one knows Who the Son is, except the Father, and Who the Father is, except the Son, and he to whom the Son wishes to reveal Him.' And turning to His taught ones He said, separately, 'Blessed are the eyes that see what you see, for I say to you that many prophets and sovereigns have wished to see what you see,** and have not seen it, and to hear what you hear, and have not heard it.'"

Who the Son is, and Who the Father is, is unknown except to **"he to whom the Son wishes to reveal."**

The greatest declaration of all, affirmed by Yahusha, is the **Shema** at Dt. 6:4, that Yahuah is one. He is alone, and there is no other. He has become your Deliverer.

Yahuah's highest attribute concerns our redemption. Yahuah has become our Deliverer, and we call on Him as our Deliverer: YAHUSHA – *I am your Deliverer.*

"ANCIENT OF DAYS" Hebrew, *ATTIQ YOMIN*

The Hebrew word ATTIQ (6268), is used to mean ancient, long ago, ANTIQUE, OLD ONE. YOM = day(s)

Rom 10:12-15:

"For there is no difference between Jew and Gentile-the same Lord is Lord of all and richly blesses all who call on him, for 'Everyone who calls on the Name of YAHUAH will be saved.' How, then, can they call on the one they have not believed in? And how can they believe in the one of whom they have not heard? And how can they hear without someone preaching (speaking) to them? And how can they preach unless they are sent? As it is written, 'How beautiful are the feet of those who bring good news!'"

At Yahukanon 17:6, Yahusha says:

"I have revealed (uncovered) Your Name to those whom You gave me out of the world."

THEY WANTED TO STOP THIS "THING"

At Acts 4, Kefa and Yahukanon had been arrested by the Sanhedrin. The elders of Yisharal were so steeped in the tradition of not saying the Name aloud, they conferred among themselves saying:

   "But to stop this thing from spreading any further among the people (the Name), we must warn these men to speak no longer to anyone in this Name." - Acts 4:17

The Name Yahusha contains the Name of Yahuah. Acts 4:7 begins their examination. Brought before the elders, Kefas and Yahukanon are asked **"By what power or by what name did you do this?"**

Ex. 23:13:

   "Be careful to do everything I have said to you. Do not invoke the names of other Alahim; DO NOT LET THEM BE HEARD ON YOUR LIPS."

For some time, Natsarim were very afraid and distrustful of Paul:

" . . . Is not this he that in Yerushaliyim made havoc of them that called on this Name? And has he come here for the intention that he might bring them bound before the chief priests?"
-Acts 9:15,16

Paul was nabbed by the Yahudim of Achaia, and they rushed him to the Roman proconsul Gallio. Gallio, a pagan, must have thought they were crazy when he heard the reason they were so murderously enraged, and he said:

"If indeed it was an act of injustice or reckless evil, O Yahudim, according to REASON I would bear with you; BUT if it be a question concerning a WORD, or NAMES, and that law which is among YOU, see you to it, for I will be no judge of THESE things." - Acts 18:14,15

ORIGIN OF THE WORD *GOD*

The *Encyclopedia Americana* (1945) says this under the topic "GOD":
"GOD (god) Common Teutonic word for personal object of religious worship, formerly applicable to super-human beings of heathen myth; on conversion of Teutonic races to Christianity, term was applied to Supreme Being."

The primary "***super-human being***" of all heathen mythology is **NIMROD**. Gen 4:26-5:1: **"At that time men began to call on the <u>Name</u> of Yahuah."** The text uses a singular form, SHEM (name), not "SHEMOTH" (names). It shows the reader the Name Yahuah. Most translators destroyed it for us.

Ex 3:13-15**: "Mosheh said to Alahim, "Suppose I go to the Yisharalites and say to them, 'The Alahim of your fathers has sent me to you,' and they ask me, 'What is His Name?' Then what shall I tell them? Alahim said to Mosheh, 'AHAYAH ASHER AHAYAH.' This is what you are to say to the Yisharalites: 'AHAYAH has sent me to you.' Alahim also said to Mosheh, 'Say to the Yisharalites, YAHUAH, the Alahim of your fathers--the Alahim of Abraham, the Alahim of Isaac and the Alahim of YaAqub--has sent me to you.' This is My Name forever, the Name by which I am to be remembered from generation to generation."**
Ex 5:2**: "Pharaoh said, 'Who is YAHUAH, that I should obey Him and let Yisharal go? I do not know YAHUAH, and I will not let Yisharal go.'"**

We are to be baptized in the NAME (not Names) - and we see at Acts 2 that singular Name is YAHUSHA, meaning "I am your Deliver."
The root *YASHA* (deliverance) is seen in the SHA and SHUA endings.
"**AMANUAL**" - *Alahim is with us*, seems to be the one exception.

This word seems to be used as a personal proper noun in 3 places: YashaYahu 7:14, 8:8, & Mt. 1:23.

This name behaves somewhat like Melchizedek, a descriptive title given to the King of Yebus, also known as Salem, a city later to become Yerushaliyim.

AMANUAL is not the Covenant Name which Yahuah has proclaimed to BE His Name.

The text says His Name (Yahuah) will be "*called*" AMANUAL.

His Name, **Yahuah**, is associated with "Alahim is with us."

Compare the personal name "JAMES BROWN" with the associated reputation that is bestowed on him: "GODFATHER OF SOUL."

In this context, we can see how AMANUEL is what Yahuah's name is "called," just as the *"Godfather of soul"* is what James Brown's name is *"called."* It's his notoriety, or giving his name a **reputation**.

It is literally "the estimation in which a person or thing is held," or the "notoriety for some particular characteristic."

At Ez. 48:35, Yerushaliyim will have the new name, "**Yahuah Shammah**."

"**Yahuah Tsedekenu**" will be proclaimed to her (YirmeYahu 33:16).

Yahusha's "new name" is prophesied to become **Yahuah Tsedekenu**:

Jer/YirmeYahu 23:6:
"In his days Yahudah will be saved and Yisharal will live in safety. This is the Name by which He will be called: Yahuah Our Righteousness."

Malaki 3:16-18:
"Then shall those who fear YAHUAH speak to one another, and YAHUAH listen and hear, and a book of remembrance be written before Him, of those who fear YAHUAH and those who think upon His Name. And they shall be Mine, said YAHUAH of armies, on the day that I prepare a treasured possession. And I shall spare them as a man spares his own son who serves him. Then you shall again see the difference between the righteous and the wrong, between one who serves Alahim and one who does not serve Him."

Mt. 10:22 tells us we will be hated because of His Name. YashaYahu 52:6 tells us that His people shall know His Name. Ezek. 20:39 says there will come a day when His Name will no longer be profaned.

"Blessed is the one coming in the Name of YAHUAH" - Ps. 118:26

This is quoted by Yahusha at Mt. 23:39:
"For I tell you, you will not see Me again until you say, 'Blessed is he who comes in the Name of Yahuah.'"

Malaki 3:16-18: **"Then those who feared Yahuah talked with one another, and Yahuah listened and heard. A scroll of remembrance was written in his presence concerning those who feared Yahuah and meditated upon his name. 'They will be mine,' says Yahuah Shaddai, 'in the day when I make up my treasured possession. I will spare them, just as in compassion a man spares his son who serves him. And you will again see the distinction between the righteous and the wicked, between those who serve Alahim and those who do not.'"**

Jer/YirmeYahu 20:9: **"But if I say, "I will not remember Him, or speak anymore in His Name,"**
Then in my heart it becomes like a burning fire shut up in my bones, and I am weary of holding it in, and I cannot endure it."

Jer/YirmeYahu 23:26-27: **"How long shall this be in the heart of the prophets that prophesy lies? yea, they are prophets of the deceit of their own heart; which think to cause My people to forget my Name by their dreams which they tell every man to his neighbour, as their fathers have forgotten my Name for Baal?"** (BAAL: Hebrew definition: LORD)

Ps 23:1: **"Yahuah** (not LORD) **is my shepherd; I shall not want."**
Invoking His Covenant Name, Yahuah declared that the Yahudim would not utter His Name:
Jer/YirmeYahu 44:24-26: **"Hear the Word of Yahuah, all you people of Yahudah in Egypt. This is what Yahuah Shaddai, the Alahim of Yisharal, says: You and your wives have shown by your actions** (making cakes, pouring drink offerings, and burning incense for ASHERAH) **what you promised when you said, 'We will certainly carry out the vows we made to burn incense and pour out drink offerings to the Queen of Heaven (ASHERAH).'**
Go ahead then, do what you promised! Keep your vows! But hear the Word of Yahuah, all Yahudim living in Egypt: 'I swear by my great Name,' says Yahuah, 'that no one from Yahudah living anywhere in Egypt will ever again invoke my Name or swear, "As surely as the Sovereign Yahuah lives."'"

WHO OR WHAT ARE YOU TOASTING TO?

We see people say, *"Let me propose a toast"* to give honors to someone with a "drink offering." To "offer a toast" comes from the ancient Babylonian custom of boasting in the name of a pagan deity, which we know now to be Nimrod. If any man boasts, what should be the reason?

Jer/YirmeYahu 9:24: **"'Let not the wise man boast of his wisdom or the strong man boast of his strength or the rich man boast of his riches, but let him who boasts boast about this:
that he understands and knows Me, that I am Yahuah, Who exercises kindness, justice and righteousness on Earth, for in these I delight,' declares Yahuah."**

Isa/YashaYahu 42:5-9: **"This is what Alahim Yahuah says - He Who created the heavens and stretched them out,
who spread out the Earth and all that comes out of it, Who gives breath to its people, and life to those who walk on it:
'I, Yahuah, have called you in righteousness; I will take hold of your hand. I will keep you and will make you to be a Covenant for the people and a light for the Gentiles, to open eyes that are blind, to free captives from prison, and to release from the dungeon those who sit in darkness.**
"I am Yahuah; that is my Name!
I will not give my glory to another or my praise to idols. See, the former things have taken place, and new things I declare; before they spring into being I announce them to you."

Many will claim His Name is not important to know. Pause and wonder! The 1611 KJV was the first time in history that anyone on this planet set eyes on the name JESUS in print. The Geneva translation had it spelled **IESVS** in 1599.

THEY WANT TO STOP "THIS THING"

The elders of Yisharal were so steeped in the tradition of not saying the Name aloud, they conferred among themselves saying:

"But to stop this thing from spreading any further among the people (the Name), we must warn these men to speak no longer to anyone in this Name." - Acts 4:17.

The Name YAHUSHA contains the Name of YAHUAH. Acts 4:7 begins their examination.

Brought before the elders, Kefa and Yahukanon are asked, **"By what power or by what name did you do this?."**

In the Talmud, unbelieving Yahudim hatefully recorded the Name of the Mashiak of Yisharal as "YESHU" often seen spelled today as "Jeschu."

Q: Where did we get the form "JESUS" from?

A: The Jesuits

The form "YESHUA" is from the acronym **YESHU**, a mutilation of Yahusha's Name used by unbelieving Yahudim during the late 1st and 2nd century CE.

The letters in YESHU stood for the sentence, *"may his name be blotted out"* (from the scroll of life). The Yeshu acronym is the root of the form "JESUS" after going through Greek, then Latin: IESU.

It's a rabbinic word-play, from the original Hebrew words:

Yemach Shmo u'Zikro. There's no letter "W" in the Hebrew alef-beth. The letter "W" is a new letter to our own alpha-beta. It's called a "DOUBLE-U" for a reason; our letter "U" is a perfect match with the sixth letter of the Hebrew alef-beth, now called a WAW, but is better rendered UAU.

Acronyms are abbreviated messages, as S.C.U.B.A. stands for **"self contained underwater breathing apparatus."**

YESU: IESOU - Going into Greek, the letter YOD became an IOTA because Greek has no "Y." The sound of "SH" was also lost, because Greek has no letters to make the sound for SH. The letter combination *OU* is a diphthong, arising from the Greek attempt to transliterate the sound "OO" as in "woof."

Our letter U and the Hebrew letter "UAU" does this easily.

YESOUS: IESOU took on an ending "S" to form IESOUS, since the Greek wanted to render the word masculine with the ending letter S. Going to Latin, the diphthong *OU* became U.

In the early 1530's the letter **J** developed, using a tail on proper names or sentences beginning with the letter i. This J is an alteration of the letter "IOTA." Many European languages pronounce J as the letter with a "Y" sound. They often spell Yugoslavia - *Jugoslavia*.

By the year 1611 the letter J was officially part of the English language, and later the King James Bible was printed with pronunciation guides for proper names like Jesus, Jew, Jeremiah, Jerusalem, Judah, James, and John.

The name "Jesus" has been in use ever since the 17th century.

TRANSLITERATION - DIFFERENT FROM TRANSLATING

All scholars know that Yahusha never heard anyone say "Jesus" to Him 2000 years ago. The letter J wasn't invented until around 1530 CE, so how could anyone get "saved" in the name "Jesus" before it was invented? To try to make it mean something in Greek, the ending "sus" definitely refers to Zeus, as it does in many other Greek names such as Tarsus, Pegasus, Dionysus, and Parnassus. So, in Greek, the Name "JEsus" can mean "hail Zeus," or "son of Zeus." It means nothing in Hebrew, the language it supposedly came from . . . But, if you force it to mean anything, the closest it could come to any Hebrew word is "the horse" because **"soos"** is Hebrew for "horse." (HE-SOOS).

The name Yeshua means "help" or "save," but the true Name **"Yahusha"** above means "I am your Deliverer." The association with Zeus with the *sus* ending is possibly an intended distortion, made by pagan copyists of long ago. Zeus was sometimes depicted as a HORSE-MAN, or centaur. The old Babylonian /Egyptian signs of the Zodiac/Zoo beasts in the skies included a centaur holding a bow and arrow, called Sagittarius - this is **Nimrod, the mighty hunter**. He was known as Orion the hunter, and later became all the solar deities of all cultures. Satan masquerades, changes, distorts, and misleads. Even "satan" came across very close to its original, *shatan*.

The translators managed to get the name for the Yerushaliyim garbage dump correct also; but they didn't try hard enough to get the Name above all names correct.

Yual 2:27-32: (QUOTED BY KEFA AT ACTS 2):

"Then you will know that I am in Yisharal -- that I am YAHUAH your Alahim, and that there is no other; never again will My people be shamed. And afterward, I will pour out my Spirit on all people. Your sons and daughters will prophesy, your old men will dream dreams, your young men will see visions.

Even on my servants, both men and women, I will pour out my Spirit in those days.

I will show wonders in the heavens and on the earth, blood and fire and billows of smoke.

The sun will be turned to darkness and the moon to blood before the coming of the great and dreadful day of YAHUAH.

And everyone who calls on the Name of YAHUAH will be saved; for on Mount Zion and in Jerusalem there will be deliverance, as YAHUAH has said, among the survivors whom YAHUAH calls."

The CRY of the Natsarim on the Hills of Afraim after their 2730-year captivity:

PSALM 80

O Hear us, Shepherd of Yisharal, You who lead Yusef like a flock, You who dwell between the kerubim, Shine Forth.

Before Afraim and Benyamin and Manasseh, stir up Your Might! Come to save us!

Turn us again, Alahim. Cause Your face to shine, and we will be saved. Yahuah Alahim Tsabaoth, How long will You be angry against the prayer of Your people? You have fed them with the bread of tears, and given them tears to drink in large measure.

You make us a source of contention to our neighbors.

Our enemies laugh among themselves. Turn us again, Alahim Tsabaoth. Cause Your face to shine, and we will be saved.

You brought a vine out of Egypt. You drove out the nations, and planted it. You cleared the ground for it.

It took deep root, and filled the land. The mountains were covered with its shadow. Its boughs were like Alahim's cedars. It sent out its branches to the sea,

Its shoots to the River. Why have You broken down its walls, so that all those who pass by the way pluck its fruit?

The boar out of the wood ravages it. The wild animals of the field feed on it.

Turn again, we beg You, Alahim Tsabaoth.

Look down from heaven, and see, and visit this vine, the stock which Your right hand planted, the branch that You made strong for Yourself. It's burned with fire. It's cut down.

They perish at Your rebuke.

Let Your hand be on the Man of Your right hand, on the Son of Adam whom You made strong for Yourself, And we shall not backslide from You. Revive us, and we will CALL on your Name. Turn us again, Yahuah Alahim Tsabaoth.

Cause Your face to shine, and we will be delivered."

Once you have seen the Truth, you can not return to the deception.

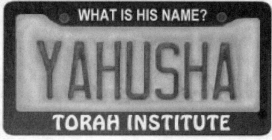

Yahusha's Name is Hebrew; not Greek, English, Chinese, or German.
Tradition is the only obstacle to accepting it.

There's an incredible amount of **witchcraft** practiced openly which few people perceive as evil in Yahusha's eyes. Instead of pledging ourselves to invisible genies, wearing wizard caps, baking cakes for the queen of heaven, lighting candles and making wishes, we need to be restored to favor with Yahusha.

Paganism is as paganism does. If we practice evil things, we will be barred from the presence of Yahusha, and not be allowed to enter through the gates of the New Yerushalayim.

"Blessed are those doing His commands, so that the authority shall be theirs unto the tree of life, and to enter through the gates into the city. But outside are the dogs and those who enchant with drugs, and those who whore, and the murderers, and the idolaters, and all who love and do falsehood." – Rev 22:14-15

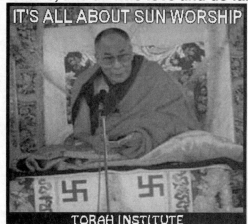

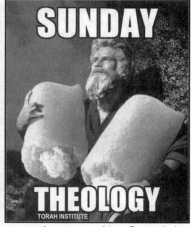

The Dalai Lama is Nimrod, as is the Pope, and every other Sun deity.

93

We've inherited only lies, and the dragon is the one being obeyed. Our enemy is not flesh and blood, and our weapons are not carnal. Our weapons are mighty in the throwing-down of strongholds (false beliefs) and all manner of false ideas, *including our speech.*
We have inherited *only* falsehood and futility – YirmeYahu 16:19.
To restore understanding to the Inspired Word, what follows is the complete *introduction* from a **Hebrew Roots translation**:

The Besorah of Yahusha - Natsarim Version (BYNV)

**"This is written for a generation to come,
so that a people to be created praise Yah."**
Tehillim - Psalms 102:18
THEY WILL NOT BE PRONE TO WORSHIP NIMROD

The **BYNV** is a *Hebrew-Roots* translation from Genesis (Barashith) to Revelation. The Name is restored to the text in Hebrew letters, while the rest of the text is in English. There are Hebrew transliterations of other names and places, and about 30 common words transliterated for those who want to learn to pronounce Hebrew without the vowel distortions introduced by the Masoretes (700's to 1100's).
The **Natsarim Writings** in this version are arranged in an order that better presents Yahusha as a Turah Teacher to the next generation. The accuracy and clarity of the message, or *besorah*, will equip us to be able to detect counterfeit ideas.
"In the beginning" [BARASHITH] is announced a *second time*, since the Natsarim Writings reflect the Light, and announce the coming of the Light. His followers warn us of a future *falling-away* from the faith. There is also a hint in Paul's writings of a future *"standing-away"* or *apostasia* which occurs in the last days.
The Natsarim of today are standing away from the false teachers, and the strongholds they have imprisoned so many minds within. His first-followers were trained in Turah observance from their childhood. In Yahusha they met the living, breathing Turah, the **Instructor Himself**. **Turah** means instruction / teaching.
Turah instructs us in how to love Yahuah, and love our neighbor. Yahusha's living obedience to the Living Words is our best guide to follow Him, and walk as He walked. The traditional mindset repels obedience, so hopefully by this new arrangement of these memoirs, new readers will first be warned against "falling away" from the Turah. The first followers were servants, and they want to teach you many things traditional teachers want you to disregard.
Open your heart, and listen to their words. **They are words of love.**

With each generation, knowledge increases concerning what was blocked or intentionally withheld. The poisoned waters are being purified with the Truth. More Light is to come, surely!

Replacement Theology:
Defiles the Everlasting Covenant, the Turah

The Christian concept known as replacement theology (or Supersessionism) proposes a "New Covenant" supersedes the Abrahimic, Moshaic, and Daudic Covenants, and the moral teachings that define sin are altered.

After the destruction of the Temple in 70 CE, a tax was imposed on the Yahudim, so very quickly the followers of Yahusha began to meet separately. They were still too similar, and so were treated the same, and taxed.

To avoid this tax, alterations were adopted so slowly almost all similarities between the Yahudim and the growing number of Gentile followers of Yahusha vanished. As we know, even their identity came to be mostly derived from Greek roots. The Hebrew roots were severed and consciously denied. You can research this early pressure to break into two factions by researching the "Jewish Tax" called **"Fiscus Judaicus."** This cause is the major reason for the early breach, and it is easily overlooked by today's teachers.

The people of Yisharal are now considered to be replaced by Christian believers, who inherit all the promises made to Yisharal. They usurp the title "Yisharal" under the label "Spiritual Israel". Engrafting to Yisharal through the **everlasting Covenant** is regarded as heresy. Reading YirmeYahu (Jer.) 31 quickly reveals the error of this thinking.

The foundation of our path must be the Word of Yahuah, and yet traditions grew up like weeds that severed all the "Hebrew roots." The pagan priesthood at Rome slowly transformed into the chimera (mixed beasts) we see, but do not perceive. One man, **Constantine I**, altered the 10 Commandments by honoring Apollo/Mithras instead of Yahuah, the Creator. His edict in 321 made "Sunday" the weekly day of rest.

The **sign** of the everlasting Covenant, Shabath, was considered "Judaizing", and anyone resting on the proper day known as "the **Sabbath**" at the Council of Laodicea (circa 365 CE) was labelled a heretic. Obeying the Shabath Command marked a person as a heretic (anathema, worthy of death). The 4th Commandment, the **sign** between Yahuah and His people forever, was directly attacked (defiled). *Rome* was the funding and enforcement, and *Alexandria* was the doctrinal center of the replacement theology. The **Didascalia**, or *Catechetical School at Alexandria*, severed all Hebrew roots through men who were harshly anti-Semitic: the **church fathers**.

Their *allegorical interpretations* made it appear that Christians replaced Yisharal, and inherited all the promises, without any obligation to obey Turah.

Turah of Yahuah also called: **Turah of Mosheh**

The Turah was given to Mosheh to teach the congregation, and the world not yet born. It is mentioned at Acts 15 in the decisions reached by the Ruach ha'Qodesh, YaAqob, Kefa, and the "chief supports" of the Natsarim. The gentiles engrafting into the Covenant were to begin with 4 main points, and continue to learn the **Turah of Yahuah**, since their parents had been idolaters. Notice this idea is expressed at Acts 15. The Turah (Mosheh) is read in the congregations, every Shabath: Act 15:21 "For from ancient generations Mosheh has, in every city, those proclaiming him – being **read** in the congregations every **Shabath**."

WHY THE EARTH WILL BE BURNED

MatithYahu 24 matches the message of YashaYahu (Isaiah) 24:5-6: **"For the earth has been defiled under its inhabitants, because they have transgressed the Turoth, changed the law, broken the everlasting Covenant. Therefore a curse shall consume the earth, and those who dwell in it be punished. Therefore the inhabitants of the earth shall be burned, and few men shall be left."**

This is one of many warnings, such as Malaki 4:4-6, and Yual 2 & 3. This is the reason the Earth will be burned in the **day of judgment**. The imaginary sacraments have been used to ensnare hearts through empty deceit, and are the **traditions** of men, Col 2.

THE RENEWED COVENANT

The "renewed Covenant" is "Mashiak in you", the promised Paraklita (Helper) that comes into our heart to inscribe His Turah on our hearts. Yahusha circumcises the hearts and minds of His followers, enabling them to receive His Mind, and to see their Teacher's point-of-view. The Natsarim, the original followers of Yahusha, realized He had come into them as He had promised.

THE FIRST-FRUITS

Those obeying the Turah of Yahuah and holding to the Testimony of Yahusha are the first-fruits, and the target of the dragon. We identify a tree by its fruit, so if we work out who has been the doctrinal source of the persecuting, we will find the servant of the dragon: the false prophet. *See also YashaYahu/Isa 13:9, 13:11, 26:21, 66:24, Mikah 5:15, ZefanYah 1:2-18, YirmeYahu/Jer 23:36*

SHEMA - Dt. 6:4-9:

Hear, O Yisharal: YAHUAH our Alahim, YAHUAH is one! And you shall love YAHUAH your Alahim with all your heart, and with all your being, and with all your might. And these Words which I am

commanding you today shall be in your heart, and you shall impress them upon your children, and shall speak of them when you sit in your house, and when you walk by the way, and when you lie down, and when you rise up, and shall bind them as a sign on your hand, and they shall be as frontlets between your eyes. And you shall write them on the doorposts of your house and on your gates."
Psalms 138:2:
I bow myself toward Your set-apart Hekal, and give thanks to Your Name for Your kindness and for Your truth; for You have made great Your Word, Your Name, above all."

TURAH OF YAHUAH

I am Yahuah your Alahim. Have no other before My Face

You do not bow to images

You do not cast the Name of Yahuah your Alahim to ruin

Remember Shabath, to keep it qodesh

You respect your father and your mother

You do not murder

You do not break wedlock

You do not steal

You do not bear false witness against your neighbor

You do not covet your neighbor's wife, house, field, servants, animals, or anything that belongs to your neighbor

Which is more correct: Jeho, Yeho, or Yahu?
We can thank the **Masoretes** (7th – 11th century "tradition-keepers") for inventing vowel-points [niqqud] to **guide** all Yahudim in the uniform pronunciation of Hebrew words. This man-made system secured one major objective: to keep the pronunciation of the Name, **Yahuah**, from **everyone's** lips. Yahusha is in His Natsarim, and He reveals the Name, and reveals the secrets that have been invented by men to

keep it held back. Many of our strongholds involve human traditions, and there are many more strongholds we must overthrow.

"YAHU"
PERSIAN COIN IN CAPTIVES' DISTRICT

ARCH OF TITUS SHOWING MENORAH

Latin letter	Value	Name of letter	Ancient	Aramaic
Y	**10**	**yod**	𐤉	י
H	**5**	**hay**	𐤄	ה
U	**6**	**uau (oo, o)**	𐤅	ו
H	**5**	**hay**	𐤄	ה

THE STONES CRY OUT FROM THE PAST

INTRODUCTION

The BYNV translation **transliterates** many original Hebrew words. The Hebrew **Name** of our Creator is preserved as written originally by the prophets in four letters, transliterated in our letters as **Yahuah.**

A **restoration** is taking place over the whole Earth.

The **key of knowledge** that was withheld in other versions is being revealed, shown on the **stone** and **coin** above.

It is the **Name "turning the world upside down"** (Acts 17:6).

At Exodus 31:18 we learn that on Mount Sinai the Creator engraved two stone tablets with His finger, and gave them to Mosheh (Moses). He engraved His Name using **four ancient vowels, in Hebrew letters: Yod-Hay-Uau-Hay**

TORAH INSTITUTE
torahzone.net

YAHUAH
YAHUSHA

Their shapes and letter names are shown in the top line above.
This Name is often represented by the letters: **YHWH**.
In their *original* form, they appeared as the Hebrew letters shown
above. This is the **Autograph** of the Creator of the universe.

   Yahuah used men to write His message to mankind in ancient
(palaeo), primary Hebrew script.
The ancient Hebrew letters sound the same, although they look
drastically different from the Aramaic script commonly seen today.
"Isaiah" 34:16 admonishes us to seek the book/scroll of **Yahuah**, and
in that scroll we find **Yahuah**'s Name written in the ancient (palaeo),
primary Hebrew. Here is a photo showing both scripts:

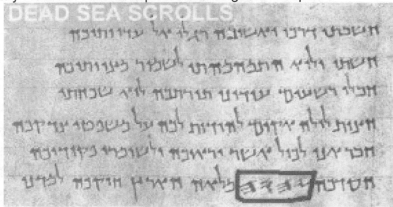

How did we come to embrace the Babylonian script (Aramaic)?
The **House of Yahudah** was taken captive to Babylon around 586
BCE. Upon their release after 70 years, they brought back the
Babylonian letter shapes which we now refer to as "modern Hebrew."
About half the book of Danial (one of the Babylonian captives) is written in
the original Hebrew, and the rest in the Babylonian script, Aramaic.
Danial was able to read the "old" script used by Yahuah when the
handwriting on the wall appeared, but the Babylonians could not [see
Danial 5]. About 400 BCE, the scribe Ezra also adopted the square
form of Babylonian Hebrew that we see today.

As scrolls would wear out, the scribes copied the scrolls in the newer Babylonian letter shapes for the general text, but one word was faithfully preserved in the original form. When they came to the Name, they carefully preserved the authentic Hebrew script. This Name is used at least 6,823 times in the TaNaK. **TaNaK** is an acronym for Turah, Nabi'im, and Kethubim, or the *Instructions, the Prophets, and the Writings.* We know that the earliest copies of the Septuagint (LXX) translation into Greek preserved the palaeo -Hebrew for **Yahuah**'s Name, whereas later copies used the Greek word *kurios* (Lord) to replace it. By replacing it, they wiped it out. From the Greek *theos* (deity) men adopted *invented terms* such as *GOD* and *god-head*.

THE SEPTUAGINT, OR LXX

The LXX transliterated the spelling of **Yahusha** (KJV: "Joshua") into the Greek letters **IESOUS** for the successor of Mosheh. Those who rely on this as evidence that it is acceptable to allow the Greek form to define the original Hebrew are simply **moving the error further into the past,** and not recognizing it as a corruption. This is a method of deception called *casuistry*. The Greek alphabet is unable to convey the correct sounds of certain Hebrew letters because it has no "SH" sound, and no letter "Y".

The third commandment in Exodus 20:7 declares we are not to *shoah* (destroy) His Name, or cast it to ruin. Yet, by denying or avoiding **Yahuah**'s Name and the Name of His Son Yahusha, both Judaism and Christianity have done exactly that, breaking the third commandment.

While in Babylon, the House of Yahudah was enslaved. They heard the Babylonians using the Name in disrespectful ways, profaning it. To help prevent this from happening, those in leadership put into effect a ban against pronouncing **Yahuah**'s Name, declaring it to be **ineffable**. By never saying the Name, it quickly became unknown to even the Yahudim. This ban is completely contrary to Scripture.

Yahuah commands us over and over again in Scripture to utter, proclaim, and **lift up** His authentic Hebrew Name. It's of paramount importance to understand that if we continue to use counterfeit names or devices for the Father and His Son, we will not be in true worship nor truly know the One we serve; we will leave ourselves open for the enemy to step in as the author of confusion, and we will be deceived. Yahusha mentioned that they had **"taken away the key of knowledge"** - Luke 11:52 - *but He was restoring it again.*

We find in Genesis 4:26 that **Yahuah**'s Name began to be called upon, and continued to be called upon up to and during the first Temple period. When the House of Yahudah was taken captive to Babylon, the Pagan Babylonian influences took a firm grip on their hearts and minds. In our modern translations, we see the result of this ban of "ineffability" in the fact that **Yahuah**'s Name has been entirely omitted, and replaced with titles, or terms which can apply to any Pagan deity, almost seven thousand times. Because the "ineffability" of the Name is not sound doctrine, the new translation you are holding restores our Father's Name and that of His Son by using the original palaeo-Hebrew script. It is found on the *Great Isaiah Scroll* among the Dead Sea Scrolls, which is now on display in the Shrine of the Book. Many ancient artifacts prove its authenticity, such as ostracons, seals, lamps, stone reliefs, and coins. By replacing the true Name into the text as it was originally written, we have done what has not been done since the first translation was made in the 2nd century BCE. This first translation from Hebrew to Greek has been named the **Septuagint**, abbreviated with the Latin letters for *seventy*: **LXX**.

Proverbs 30:4 asks us a weighty question, "...What is His Name, and what is His Son's Name..." Rabbinical Judaism calls **Yahuah** by the substitute terms, *HaShem, Adonai or Alahim* - none of which are His Name; they are *titles or pronouns.* In Christianity, they use "Jehovah" for the Father and "Jesus" for the Son, both of which are not authentic. They are imprinted with the corruptions found in the Greek and Latin alphabets. The Names can't be "Jehovah" or "Jesus", because there is no letter "**J**" in Hebrew (the letter "J" appeared on Earth during the 16th century). The Greek added the ending letter "S" to the Name of Yahusha.

ORIGIN OF WORD "GOD"

We learn that Yahuah removed His Name from our lips during the captivity in Babel [see YirmeYahu 44:26]. The device "LORD" has been embraced to refer to Yahuah. Another term, *GOD*, has come to replace the original Hebrew word "Alahim."

Read Exodus 23:13 right now. With that Scripture in mind, consider the following reference:

The ***Encyclopedia Americana*** (1945 Edition) says under the topic *GOD*: **GOD** (god); **"Common Teutonic word for personal object of religious worship, formerly applicable to super-human beings of heathen myth; on conversion of Teutonic races to Christianity, term was applied to Supreme Being."**

1 Thessalonians 5:22 warns us not to give the appearance of evil, and this would have to include what comes from our mouths. Guile is deceit. When we speak guile using replacement names, or use titles in place of His Name, we are breaking the third commandment and giving the appearance of evil in our speech. We are **circumlocuting** *(talking around)* the Name, but not really saying it. *"He knows who we mean"* is the common response. Many say they don't use the Name because they want to keep from offending people. They don't mind offending Yahuah; He knows *"their heart."*

LORD IN HEBREW IS BAAL?

Numbers 6:24-27 reveals **Yahuah**'s Name will be upon His people: What Name would that be, the **LORD**? Again, in Genesis 4:26 we learn that men began to call upon **Yahuah**'s Name. There is only one Name given under heaven (Acts 4:12). In 1 Kings 18:24 we find that Aliyahu/Elijah called on the Name of **Yahuah** while the Pagans called on the names of their deities (Baal and Asherah); clearly there must be a distinction in what we call our Creator. **Baal** in Hebrew means "**lord.**" LORD is not the true name we should be calling upon.

Deuteronomy 28:10 reveals that all nations will see that we are called by **Yahuah**'s **Name.** Revelation 22:4 reveals that **Yahuah**'s Name will be on our foreheads: So, what name do we want on (or in) our foreheads? Malaki 3:16 commands us to think upon **Yahuah**'s Name, but historically neither Judaism nor the *Kirche* have been thinking on His true Hebrew Name. Micah 4:5 reveals that we are to walk in **Yahuah**'s Name. In Psalms 83:16-18 **Yahuah** commands us to seek His Name. Psalms 72:17 tells us that **Yahuah**'s Name will endure forever, but Judaism and the Kurk (Kirke, or Circus, the original term for a Pagan place of worship) have placed a stumbling block where His Name is concerned. Not only have they both forgotten His Name but they have "destroyed" **Yahuah**'s Name thousands and thousands of times in Scripture. The Hebrew term for the "called-out" is the QAHAL, and today we think of the assembly, as well as a meeting place, as a "kurche" - **KIRKE**, the **Greek** term for a Pagan Temple, and derived from the name of a witch, **CIRCE,** sometimes rendered "KIRCHE" in English.

Regarding praise and worship, we are told in 2 Samuel 7:26 that we are to magnify **Yahuah**'s Name, but in reality we have been magnifying unscriptural names and mere titles that might apply to any generic, non-specific deity. Psalms 106:47 declares that we are to give thanksgiving to **Yahuah**'s Name, but clearly we've been giving thanksgiving to foreign names. Psalms 29:2 says we are to esteem **Yahuah**'s Name. Psalms 9:2 declares that we are to sing praises to **Yahuah**'s Name. Isaiah 56:6 reveals that we are to **love Yahuah**'s Name. Psalms 45:17 tells us that every generation is to remember **Yahuah**'s Name. Exodus 3:14,15 declares His memorial Name to all generations is **Yahuah.**

Salvation is found in **Yahuah**'s Name and that of His Son, Yahusha, (Ps 54:1; Joel 2:32 and Acts 2:21; 4:12). We are to call on **Yahuah**'s Name in the Name of His Son for deliverance. Are we to use counterfeit names or common titles when we pray for redemption?

Using a personal name is a matter of *identification*. Pronouncing a person's name as accurately as we can is a sign of respect. Men have hidden, disguised, corrupted, and substituted the Name of our Creator.

"Jehovah" and "Jesus" are of recent origin.

THE NAME JEHOVAH

Instead of Jehovah, the Name appeared as **Iehoua** in the *Geneva translation*, and in the first printings of the KJV. In subsequent printings of the KJV, the letter "J" began to be used for the first letter of proper nouns that began with the letter "I", and at the beginning of sentences. The letter "J" is but a few hundred years old. What's startling though is this: when Jehovah is broken down we have "Je hovah" with the "Je" replacing His shortened, poetic name "Yah." "HOVAH" is referenced in **Strong's Exhaustive Concordance** as word H1943, and means lay-waste, destruction, or ruin. When we speak the hybrid name "Jehovah", we are in essence saying "Yah, He is ruin." Another perspective, perhaps closer to the truth, is how letters changed their sounds over recent centuries. The letter shaped "V" we see used over 400 years ago is the old Latin shape that functioned as our modern letter "U". Note the word GLADIVS in its old form utilizes the "V" SHAPE, but it SOUNDED like our modern letter "U". Because of this distortion, the spelling JEHOVAH has been misunderstood. To correctly understand the pronunciation, the "J" sounds like a "Y", and the "V" sounds like a "U". The "OU" (or "OV") is simply a diphthong, making the word really sound like "Ya-Hoo-ah", so the *ovah* portion would be improved for today by writing it *ouah*. This produces Yah+ *ouah*. The transliteration (trans-lettering) of many words and names is being better understood when these obstacles are removed.

An early transliteration of the Name Yahuah into Greek used the letters **IAOUE**. It was Clement of Alexandria (a headmaster of the **Didascalia**, the **Catechetical School of Alexandria**, Egypt) who first demonstrated a trans-lettering effort for the pronunciation of the Name using **Greek** letters, **IAOUE.**

The name "Jesus" has only been around for the last few hundred years. The "J" appeared on the planet less than 500 years ago, so clearly we've been using a mutated form of the original Name for our Savior. The Name "Yahusha" (I am your Deliverer) was given to Yusef in a dream, not the name "Jesus." Those who cling to the recent form "Jesus" and will not listen to reason must ask themselves, "*what does that mean for all those believers who never used "Jesus" prior to the 16th century?*" Where's the respect for the Names of the Almighty and His Son, the same respect that we demand for our own personal names?

Some feel they can call the Father and His Son by any name of their choosing, yet they feel that **Yahuah** should have their name correct in the *Scroll of Remembrance*, or the Lamb's *Scroll of Life* (whichever scroll it may appear in). Clearly, there is a double-standard toward **Yahuah's** Name and that of His Son, **Yahusha**. Men are not endowed with the authority to choose whatever name they prefer to call upon for their salvation, they must submit to Truth, and build on what does not change.

We are told in Isaiah 52:6 that **Yahuah**'s people will "know" His Name. Revelation 3:8 warns us that we are not to deny His Name. Jeremiah 10:25 reveals to us that **Yahuah** will pour out His wrath on those who do not call on His Name. It would be an act of rebellion to ignore these clear instructions; they are not suggestions. ZekarYah 13:9 tells us that those who belong to **Yahuah** will say, "**Yahuah** is the Name of my Alahim." The traditions of our fathers have failed us in this regard. We are told in Revelation 2:13 that we are to hold fast to His Name, but men have not preserved the Truth; it has fallen in the streets. Why did the Prushim and Priests tell Yahusha's followers not to utter His Name? Because they knew that when Yahusha's Name was being uttered that the Father's Name was being uttered as well because the Father's Name is in His Son, Exodus 23:21.

EXCUSES

Let's examine some of the excuses people use to reject the true Name. Some declare that **Yahuah** has *many* names. No, **Yahuah** has **one** Name and many offices, such as Healer, Shepherd, Redeemer, Father, Husband, Protector, Possessor of Heaven and Earth, etc. Some claim that no matter what name they use, **Yahuah** will know who they mean. This excuse boasts of prideful arrogance, implying that the Creator of Shamayim and Arets will just have to figure it out and deal with the terms **we** choose. It's as if we're naming Him, yet we have no such authority. He'll have to take what we dish out, and like it? Others say that the pronunciation of **Yahuah**'s Name has been lost. Do we really believe, even for one moment, that **Yahuah** is going to command us to CALL (*QARA*) upon His Name and then allow the pronunciation to be lost? *Of course not.* All we must do is "sound-off" the letters; surely we can trust in the most-used word in all of Scripture. The Dead Sea Scrolls have revealed many examples of the original letter form which the Words of Yahuah were written in. Some proclaim that **Yahuah**'s Name is not found in the **Brith Kadasha**.

The reason we don't see **Yahuah**'s Name in the Brith Kadasha is because it has been replaced, and it became *policy* to adopt alternate, "popular" terms as *substitutions* for it. Titles are not names.

THE FATHER'S NAME – 4 vowels

Now let's examine the pronunciation of the Father's name. The 1st century writer called "Josephus" tells us that the Name consists of "*four vowels*". Commonly we see the Name in encyclopedias as **YHWH**. These vowel-letters stand for the Hebrew letters: Yod, Hay, Uau, and Hay. The Yod is the same as our letter "Y." The Hay is the same as the letter "H", and the Uau is often waw, represented as the *double-u,* but is essentially the sound of "oo." The letter *Hay* appears as the second and fourth letter.

The Assyrians heard and transcribed the proper transliteration of our Father's Name as Ya-u-a (Yahuah). Having lived with the Israelites who had been taken into captivity by the Assyrians, their transliteration is then creditable. The state of IOWA is said to be based on the Name, handed-down through the native-American tribes. These tribes were remnants of the explorers sent by Solomon to establish *colonies* and mine copper, tin, silver, iron, and gold.

Concerning Josephus, the first-century historian, we read in his book *Josephus Complete Works*, p. 556, that *he had observed the priestly headpiece*. On this headpiece the Father's Name consisted of *four vowels*. The first two vowel-letters are "Yod Hay" and according to Strong's #H3050 it is pronounced as "Yah." We find an example of this shortened, poetic form of Yahuah's name in Psalms 68:4. We can see these letters are vowels even as they are used in English. When we say "Y" we can hear the "i" sound. When we pronounce the "H," we can hear the "a" sound because the "h" is silent, as seen with the name *Sarah*.

Now we come to the third vowel-letter **Uau**, often erroneously rendered Vav/Waw. The UAU is the vowel-letter sound "oo." It is not pronounced as our letter "W," since the Hebrew alef beth does not have a letter to correspond to our W. *The letter W first appeared in the 13th century.* It should not be thought of as a "double" anything; it's simply a "**U**." Now we have two syllables: "YaH + U," *YAHU.*

The Masoretes altered this with invented vowel markings so it became YEHO, to misdirect anyone from uttering the Name correctly.

The fourth letter of the Name is the vowel-letter *Hay*. Some believe that the ending of Yahuah's Name has an *-ah* and others *-eh*.

The Tribe of *Yahudah* gives us a significant clue.

The Name YAHUDAH is spelled: Yod-Hay-Uau-Daleth-Hay.

If we remove the "Daleth" which is a "D," we find the four letters, **Yod-Hay-Uau-Hay.**

YAHUDAH – minus the D = YAHUAH

Is it possible to find this truth in the Greek? **Josephus** (Flavius Yusef, born Yusef Ben Matithyahu, 37-101 CE, a Yahudi historian) confirms that our Father's Name consisted of 4 vowels, with the UAU having the "oo" sound which agrees with the Assyrian pronunciation *Ya-u-a*, and is pronounced **YAHUAH.**

Strong's #H3068 (6823 entries) renders Yahuah's name as *Yehovah*, which is inaccurate. Checking H3050 we find that His shortened, poetic name, **YaH**, refers us right back to H3068, which which they rendered as "Yeh..." **Yah** is correct; **Yeh** is an alteration. The **Yeh** spelling is the result of the **Masoretes**, who used alternative vowels from another word, **adonai**, in order to keep the Name of Yahuah concealed from the masses, thus *perpetuating the ban of pronouncing the Name aloud.* The vowel-pointing by the Masoretes cannot be trusted because of their intention to hide the Name of our Father, **Yahuah**. The vowels they used were intended to direct the reader to say **ADONAI** instead of what was written - it was to "cue" the reader to not pronounce the Name! In the Name Yahusha, "Ya/Yah" was changed to "Ye/Yeh" which hides the connection with the Name of the Father, Exodus 23:21.

For further confirmation we read in The ***Stromata***, v. 6, by Clement of Alexandria: **"...the mystic name of the four letters which was affixed to those alone to whom the *adytum was accessible, is called 'IAOUE' which is interpreted, *'Who is and shall be.'"***
[An **adytum was the innermost sanctuary of an ancient Greek temple]*

How then does "ahayah - I Am" fit into our understanding of Father's Name? At Exodus 3:14 we read, "... ahayah Asher ahayah: and He said, 'This shall you say to the children of Yisharal, ahayah has sent me to you.'" **Ahayah asher ahayah** means *"I will be Who I will be."* When Father spoke "ahayah Asher ahayah," He was speaking of Himself in the first-person because only He can claim *"I will be,"* whereas when He reveals to His people that His Name is Yahuah, He is speaking in the third-person. **Yahuah** is the Name we are to know, declare, and worship through the Name **Yahusha**, **Yah** (is) **our Deliverer,** or **I am your Deliverer**.
He identifies Himself exclusively by this **one Name.** Yahusha clearly tells us in John 17:26 that He had declared His Father's Name to the people and since we are Yahusha's body, we are to do the same, Colossians 1:18. How foolish to think that the Head, Yahusha would call His Father **Yahuah** (Yahuah), but His body (us) would call our Father, LORD, God or Jehovah makes no sense, does it?
How can Yahuah's Name be "Jehovah" and the Son's Name be "Jesus" since there is no "J" in Hebrew?
The apostle "John" is really "Yahukanon." At John (Yahukanon) 5:43 Yahusha tells us that He came in His Father's Name. He came in the authority of Yahuah, and carries this Name in His own.
Jeremiah (YirmeYahu) 23:25-27 tells us that lies have caused **Yahuah**'s people to forget His Name for **BAAL**, meaning "**LORD.**"

Many faulty interpretations have been propagated through the leadership in both Judaism and Christianity. Not only have Judaism and Christianity replaced the Names of the Father and His Son, but they've even changed the original palaeo-Hebrew names of the prophets in order to conceal **Yahuah**'s Name because this Name is embedded in the original names of several prophets. An example of this is found in the name of the prophet known as "Jeremiah."

In Hebrew his name contains the shortened, poetic form of Father's Name, "**Yah**" and should have been transliterated as *Yirme Yahu* (see any concordance). Notice that it ends with "Yah."

The word "Isaiah" should be rendered *YashaYahu*. Notice the ending "**iah**" in these two names. These prophets would not recognize their own names as they are found in our modern-day, English Scriptures.

THE SON'S NAME

Hebrews 13:8 tells us that Yahusha is the same yesterday, today and forever. So do we really believe that He has changed His Name from Hebrew to a Greco/Roman/English name? Of course not. And we learn from Philippians 2:9 that His Name is above every name. Would that include His Father's Name? No, it wouldn't, and here's why: again, Exodus 23:21 tells us that the Father's Name is in His Son. The Father and His Son share the shortened, poetic name "Yah." Acts 4:12 tells us there is no other name by which we can be delivered. That name in true Hebrew is:

Yod-Hay-Uau-Shin-Ayin: *Yahusha*

This script is read *right-to-left*. Notice that the first three vowel-letters are exactly the same as the Father's name "**Yahu**." Next we have the letter "shin" which is "sh," and finally the Ayin which is sometimes silent or represented by a rough breathing sound in the back of the throat.

The Greco/Roman/English name *Jesus* would have been unknown to Yahusha. *Jesus* has no meaning in Hebrew, whereas Yahusha means *Yah is our Deliverer*, or *I am your Deliverer*. The one who hung on the stake/tree for us was named Yahusha not someone named Jesus. Why is it that most believers readily accept the free gift of His finished work at Golgatha, but refuse to acknowledge Him by His Hebrew Name which was given to Him by His Father, **Yahuah**? Clearly, we are to call on His Hebrew Name for salvation but regretfully that has not been the case in the Kirche (Church).

IESU was the Latin form from 391 to the 16th century. Arabs were influenced during the 7th century by this form, and refer to Yahusha as *ISA*. **ISA** taken back into Hebrew becomes **ESU**, the name of YaAqob's brother, **ESAU**, a word meaning *hairy*.

If we take a closer look at the original Hebrew name for Joshua, we find that it is the clearest example of how our Mashiak's Name is spelled and pronounced. Strong's #H3091 spells Joshua's name in Hebrew as "**Yod Hay Uau Shin Ayin**," this is exactly how we spell Yahusha's Name today. Some add another UAU after the SHIN, which is perfectly acceptable. *[compare **YARUSHA** at 2Mal. 15:33]*

Here's something very enlightening: if we look up the name "Jesus" in Strong's #G2424 it is sounded out as "ee-ay-sooce," but refers us right back to Joshua in Strong's #H3091 "Yeh ho shua." For further proof, we go to Acts 7:45, where we find the name Joshua in our English

Scriptures, but what's amazing is that it is the exact same number in Strong's #G2424 which is used for the name "Jesus."

Names are always transliterated from the source language to the target language by their sounds. Names have meanings, but it is not proper to translate them; In short, names are transliterated by the sound of each letter no matter what the alphabets used may be, just as our own name in English will always sound the same no matter what foreign alphabet it may encounter.

What do we do with the alternative spellings such as *Y'shua, Yeshua or Yahshua*? Some claim that Y'shua or Yeshua is the shortened, *Aramaic* form for His Name. Others declare that Yeshua is a form of **Yeshu**, an unscriptural acronym for Yahusha's Name and stands for **Ye**mak **Sh**mo **U'**Zikro, meaning *may his name be blotted out.* So we can see why this would be a name that the enemy would like us to use because every time we speak Yeshua, we are in essence declaring that His Name be blotted out. The form Yah_shua leaves out the "uau" which is the vowel-letter sound "oo." 2 Timothy 2:15 tells us we are to "rightly divide the word of truth", so what has been hidden or **whispered** in secret is now being **shouted** from the rooftops.

We learn at Acts 9:15 that Shaul/Paul was to bear Yahusha's Name before the nations. It is impossible for Paul to have declared the Greco/Roman/English name "Jesus". Shaul declared the Name of **Yahusha**; and as His body, so must we. Shaul was sent to arrest and kill those who called upon the true Name. Following his own conversion to the Truth of the Name (by Yahusha Himself), he used it boldly and was stoned several times for it.

They wouldn't have stoned him if he had used the name of error we have inherited. In conclusion, we must make a choice.

How long do we waver between two opinions?

If Yahuah is Alahim, then serve Him; if Baal (Lord) is Alahim, serve him. Do we call our Creator and His Son by unreal names and common titles which Rabbinical Judaism and Christianity have traditionally deceived us with, or do we return to the ancient, palaeo-Hebrew written by the finger of **Yahuah** / **YaHUaH**? If Scripture is the final authority in our lives, then the answer is very clear. Scripture reveals **Yahuah** / YaHUaH and Yahusha's correct identity through the palaeo-Hebrew Names and it's upon this foundation that we must stand firmly. Yahusha revealed that **He** is "Al Shaddai" at Revelation 1:8, explaining the mysterious use of the identity marker, **ALEF-TAU** throughout the TaNaK. Yahuah is "ONE," and He became flesh and dwelled among us in the form of a man. The Name is the *Key of knowledge* which has been withheld from us, and it will unlock the revealed Word to any who accept it, giving understanding and wisdom to the simple. Yahusha has revealed His identity through the ALEF-

TAU revelation. The very idea there is a "key" validates that there is something to be *unlocked.*

That would be the Besorah, the *message* of Yahusha. He said He would be with us, and only ONE Being is capable of being in more than one place at once. Now you know Who the Father is, and Who the Son is.

This book is His message to all mankind, to teach us how to love Him, and love one another.

THE MESSAGE OF LOVE

The Besorah is the *message* given to prophets selected by the Creator Being, YAHUAH (**Yahuah**) to all mankind. This *message* is both a record of specific events, and a revelation of the plan of redemption and restoration. The original parents of all mankind were perfect, created to live in "Eden" (bliss, delight), and they were deathless. They were deceived by a fallen creature that brought doubt into believing the Word of **Yahuah**, and so they failed a simple test of faith in what He had spoken. Through this error, *death entered the world.* *Life* and *death* are on display throughout the entire message, and **Yahuah** calls out to all men to *choose life*, by believing in His Word, and proving they believe it by *obeying* Him. This choice is made by having faith in His Word, the message (Hebrew, *besorah*), and living by it, according to the Covenant given to a chosen people He selected (Yisharal, aka Israel).

THIS TRANSLATION IS DIFFERENT

Former translations, such as the 1611 KJV, were done by scholars who believed the Earth was flat, and the sun circled it; Galileo went on trial in 1633 for his ideas about the Earth circling the sun. Theologically, this doesn't matter because eternal life is not denied due to being misinformed about the shape of the Earth or what we think orbits what. More importantly, the scholars held to the teachings of the **church fathers**, and the poisonous wormwood of Replacement Theology. This will be discussed briefly at the end of this introduction. Whatever translation you may own, check Mt. 26:17 and Mark 14:12. If it reads ***"On the first day of unleavened bread"*** they used the KJV for their framework. You can't look for a place to observe Passover when it's already happened. The 1st day of Matsah is the 15th day of the 1st moon, Passover lambs were killed on the 14th. There is no word "day" used here. The word *protos* should have been understood as "***prior to*** Matsah (Unleavened Bread)."

More importantly, the *personal Name* of the Creator is deleted from most English translations, substituted with the word "LORD", and in some cases the word "GOD".

In this version, the true Name is restored in its original form in the places it occurs in the inspired text, and other names are more accurately transliterated, eliminating the distortions caused by the Greek and Latin alphabets. Greek terms such as "Genesis" and "Exodus" are accompanied by the authentic Hebrew terms. Hebrew is the *lashon qodesh*, or *set-apart tongue*, so restoring the names without distortion enables the reader to experience the richness, purity, and authenticity that flows from the unfiltered, inspired words in the Creator's Mind. The *key of knowledge* is the personal Name of the Creator, and using it unlocks the message that would otherwise remain sealed from our comprehension. A name uniquely identifies who is being spoken of. The first known *translation* of Yahuah's Word was made from Hebrew into the Greek language between 285-246 BCE for a Ptolemaic king at Alexandria, Egypt. That translation is often referred to as the Septuagint, or the Latin designation, LXX.

Septuagint is Latin for "seventy", as traditionally it was assumed that 70 scribes were used to translate the **Turah** (5 books of Mosheh) into Greek. When they did so, they left the Name of the Most High Alahim unmolested, **as this translation also does.** So, what you are holding in your hands is one of the few times since the **LXX** that a translation has been made that leaves the original Name as it appeared in the Hebrew. Lies inherited from our fathers will be overcome with Truth.

THE SCRIPT IN ITS HISTORICAL CONTEXT

An alphabet may be different than that of the language it conveys. You are reading English words (the language), but those words are written in Latinized letters. A word may be Hebrew, such as "Shabath", but is written here in Latinized letters. When the Yahudim were taken to Babel, they adopted a foreign alphabet, Aramaic. It is mis-named "modern Hebrew." The Hebrew alphabet is mistakenly called "Phoenician."

The original autograph of the Creator is best shown using the ancient, primary letters He used to write His Name with His finger at Sinai. The world has called this letter style *Phoenician*, not realizing that the label, *Phoenician*, was bestowed upon the Israelites by the Greek writers, a word meaning *date palm* in Greek. The word **Phoenix** (Latin *poenus*) means the same thing. The Roman Empire converted this word to *Punic* when they were battling their "Israelite" enemies at Carthage. The **Yisharalites** have been called many things by the land empires over the ages, such as *Carthaginians, Parthians, or Scythians;* but as *Phoenicians* they are described to be *sea people*. The Yisharalites dwelled in the land given to them by Yahuah, however they were far more of a *sea empire* than a *land empire*. When you see sources describing the true Hebrew script as *Phoenician*, you can better understand that this term applies to the *Yisharalite* empire made up of many colonies. Herodotus coined the word "Phoenician."

111

The Yisharalites made alliances with Tyre and Sidon, causing the northern 10 tribes to fall into Baal worship, and for this they were scattered into the nations by the Assyrian empire (circa 722 BCE).

The Israelites called the land "Canaan" before they conquered it, and a small part of it was known as **"Philistia"**, which the Romans later adopted into their form, **Palestine**. It is commonly thought that the Israelites adopted their alef-beth (alphabet) from the residents of Canaan (Byblos, Tyre, Sidon), but the reverse is the case. The Semitic language and 22-lettered alef-beth was common to all descendants of Shem. Shem gives us the term **Shemite**, losing the "sh" sound by passing through the Greek language, and becoming *"Semite."*

WHAT IS THE MESSAGE?

The **Besorah** is the answer to mankind's oldest mystery, the purpose of life: *to learn to love*.

Active love is **serving**. From beginning to end, the Creator has pleaded, searched hearts, and repeated Himself beyond measure for mankind to return to Him. Who has ears to hear Him? He said, **"Love Me, and guard My Commandments."**

The Word, Light, Wisdom, Living Water, and His Covenant are all the same thing: the **Turah of Yahuah**. Turah teaches **how** to love.

Without love, Creation has no purpose.

The Mashiak of Israel, Yahusha of Natsarith, told an elder of Israel:

"If you do not believe when I spoke to you about earthly things, how are you going to believe when I speak to you about the heavenly things?

And no one has gone up into the heavens except He who came down from the heavens – the Son of Adam. And as Mosheh lifted up the serpent in the wilderness, even so must the Son of Adam be lifted up, so that whosoever believes in Him should not perish but possess everlasting life. For Alahim so loved the world that He gave His only procreated Son, so that everyone who believes in Him should not perish but possess everlasting life.

For Alahim did not send His Son into the world to judge the world, but that the world through Him might be saved. He who believes in Him is not judged, but he who does not believe is judged already, because he has not believed in the Name of the only procreated Son of Alahim.

And this is the judgment, that the light has come into the world, and men loved the darkness rather than the light, for their works were evil. For everyone who practices evil hates the light and does not come to the light, lest his works should be exposed. But the one doing the truth comes to the light, so that his works are clearly seen, that they have been wrought in Alahim." – Yn. 3

"**And He Himself is an atoning slaughter for our sins, and not for ours only but also for all the world. And by this we know that we know Him, if we guard His Commands. The one who says, 'I know Him,' and does not guard His Commands, is a liar, and the truth is not in him. But whoever guards His Word, truly the love of Alahim has been perfected in him. By this we know that we are in Him: The one who says he stays in Him ought himself also to walk, even as He walked. Beloved, I write no recent command to you, but an original Command which you have had from the beginning. The original Command is the Word which you heard from the beginning.**" - 1 Yahukanon (**Turah** is the original Command)

DAVID, DAWID, OR DAUD?

The contemporary English spelling of this great ruler is **David**, and often people say "**da-VEED**" or "da-WEED" thinking this is a more modern Hebrew posture.

Modern Hebrew is different in some aspects from the authentic 22 letters. The 6th letter, **UAU**, has morphed into WAW. The influences of foreign languages have caused this letter to become a VAV, but it is simply a **U**. This name is spelled with 3 letters, DALETH-UAU-DALETH, or literally **D-U-D** in our English.

The Hebrew letters DALETH-UAU-DALETH will be transliterated **Daud**, to suggest the pronunciation **da-OOD**.

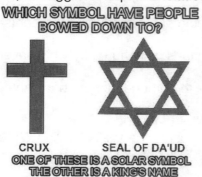

WHICH SYMBOL HAVE PEOPLE BOWED DOWN TO?

CRUX   SEAL OF DA'UD

ONE OF THESE IS A SOLAR SYMBOL
THE OTHER IS A KING'S NAME

The Name **Yahuah** is associated with His **Word**, and He guards His Covenant. The menorah is physically a LIGHT with **seven branches**. The seven lamps can be abstractly thought of as His eyes, as we contemplate His perspective of how all mankind should live. The menorah also shows us the 7 festivals which represent the process of redemption. These annual observances are **shadows** of how Yahuah is redeeming His bride, Yisharal (Israel).

The inspired Word gives us mankind's true history.

As you read it, you are actually reading the very thoughts of your Creator. Take His heart into yours as you read.

He wants you to know the Truth, and how much He has done for you. We who are followers of Yahusha are being healed as if we were in a "Natsarim hospital." Hopefully, we see improvement each day.
Here is a modern parable about how we should consider one another.

THE TOUCH

Parables are "dark sayings." The meaning of the components is hidden so that comprehension is not possible for outsiders to interpret the parable properly. The components of a parable, when properly revealed, enable the hearer to interpret the meaning.

MEANING OF SYMBOLS IN THIS PARABLE
HALLMARK: Outward sign or signal, family crest, primary trait
NAME: The identity that specifically defines someone apart from all others
LEPER: a sinner, slowly dying a horrible death; and this represents every person in the world
LIGHT: Torah, the Words; the instructions of Yahuah, by which every person is to live by
PHYSICIANS: The general reference to human teachers of all anti-Torah patterns
THE PHYSICIAN: Yahusha, the Light of the world
TOUCH: Indwelling of the Spirit of Yahusha, the Well of Living Waters

THE TOUCH – *of the Physician*
A land was filled with many leprous people, all having spent their wealth on physicians that could not heal them. They were hopeless, and turned away from all physicians, considering them to be frauds. As one of the lepers lay dying, he prayed a final prayer that someone be sent to help the others to be cured and live normal healthy lives. Immediately, a brilliant Light enveloped him, and a kind Presence came into him. The Light brought him joy, peace, and healing. He realized that Yahusha, the Creator of all things, had healed him because he prayed for others, not himself.
He had learned to love others more than his own life, and had been begotten from above by the Touch of the Physician.

114

Rising up in complete health of mind and body, the former leper went to share what had happened to him, and told everyone the Name of Yahusha healed him. Each leprous person who accepted the Name of Yahusha received the healing Light, and arose to continue the work of sharing the Name of the Physician, Who delivers from death, and is the Light of Life.

Certain lepers who would not accept the Words and receive the Light became bitter and envious, and began to malign the former lepers who worked among the leper community. They accused them of all kinds of shameful activities, evidenced by the fact they associated with known lepers.

As more and more healthy people heard about the work among the lepers, support for their work came in from all over the world.

Kindness, encouragement, and love propelled a great restoration.

Love became the hallmark between all those who accepted the Light, and they gave praise and honor to the touch of The Physician that took away the leprosy of death, and brought His Life into the darkness of a dying world.

Yn. 3:16-21: **"For Alahim so loved the world that He gave His only brought-forth Son, so that everyone who believes in Him should not perish but possess everlasting life.**

For Alahim did not send His Son into the world to judge the world, but that the world through Him might be saved.

He who believes in Him is not judged, but he who does not believe is judged already, because he has not believed in the Name of the only brought-forth Son of Alahim.

And this is the judgment, that the Light has come into the world, and men loved the darkness rather than the Light, for their works were wicked. For everyone who is practicing evil matters hates the Light and does not come to the Light, lest his works should be exposed. But the one doing the truth comes to the Light, so that his works are clearly seen, that they have been wrought in Alahim."

THE NIMROD MATRIX

The first man to be worshipped as a **"mighty-one"** (GOD) was Nimrod. The World Order is a scheme to make everyone compliant to a Nimrod Matrix, or mode of conduct.

If we are worshipping Yahuah, we are obeying His Commandments. **If we are worshipping the Nimrod Matrix, we are working much harder.** We are running into a steeple every week to pay someone to tell us we don't have to obey, baking birthday cakes, lighting candles and making wishes, boasting blessings with lifted beverages, carving pumpkins and dressing up for the witchfest, erecting trees in our homes pretending it's not about the Sun's birth, coloring eggs and eating chocolate rabbits, decorating the outside of our home with lights, pretending that an authority figure has power "vested in them" to pronounce us married (when it was Yahuah alone Who joined us together in marriage), and so on.

If you look through your family photos, they tend to involve occasions the Nimrod Matrix has obliged us to **swarm**. Stop swarming on the traditional occasions, and the family bonds are wounded severely.

"And He answering, said to them,
"Well did Yashayahu prophesy concerning you hypocrites, as it has been written, 'This people respect Me with their lips, but their heart is far from Me.
And in vain do they worship Me, teaching as teachings the commands of men.' Forsaking the Command of Alahim, you hold fast the tradition of men."
And He said to them, "Well do you set aside the command of Alahim, in order to guard your tradition." - Mark 7:6-9

With Yahusha's words in mind, what **traditions** have come to replace the Commands of Yahuah? Christmas; Easter; Sunday; Halloween (feast of dead saints); sacraments; steeples; bells; crosses; eating unclean animals; apostolic succession; celibacy; veneration of human remains, images; holy water; indulgences; trinitarian ideas; prayer beads; prohibition of true Name, Yahuah, Yahusha; prayers to the dead (necromancy); infant baptism; and much more.

Men have set aside the Commands of Yahuah for their traditions.

THE SIGN OF YUNAH: 3 Days, 3 Nights, Yunah, and Yahusha

A sign can be a gesture of assurance, or a mark of authenticity that proves something to be true. Yahusha was asked a question by the scribes and Pharisees concerning His authority to teach (Mt. 12:38-40):

"Then some of the scribes and Pharisees answered, saying, 'Teacher, we wish to see a sign from You.' But He answering, said to them, 'A wicked and adulterous generation seeks after a sign, and no sign shall

116

be given to it except the sign of the prophet Yunah. For as Yunah was three days and three nights in the stomach of the great fish, so shall the Son of Adam be three days and three nights in the heart of the earth.'"

People have misunderstood how Yahusha was in the heart of the Earth for *"three days and three nights"* because they think "preparation day" only refers to their day called "Friday." When understood within the context of Yisharal rather than Christianity, the "preparation day" referred to at Mt. 27:62, Mk. 15:42, Lk. 23:54, and Yn. 19:31 is the day before the mo'ed (appointed time) of Matsah. This preparation is for the fifteenth day of the first moon. Passover lambs were slain on the preparation day, the 14th.

ABIB 15

This fifteenth day is an annual Shabath (rest day), so the ***14th of every first moon is always termed a "preparation day."*** The Greek text captures the idea of the approaching day as a "High" Shabath in the word "MEGAS" (G3173), Yn. 19:31.
This has nothing to do with the *SHABUA* (week) of 7 days, **only the moon.**

The opinion that the term *preparation day* is always implying a Friday is an error. The actual day of the week is irrelevant. we know the day Yahusha was impaled was the 4th day of the week, several hours after sunrise.
This was the Roman/Celtic day called *"Woden's-Daeg."*
Carefully counting the days and nights from the time Yahusha was entombed, we find the following chain of events:
Nakdimon and Yusef took Yahusha's body from the tree at the close of the day, just prior to sunset, because at the approaching sunset was the first day of **Matsah** (Unleavened Bread) Abib 15, a "high" day:
Woden's-Daeg at sunset began night 1; the next sunrise began the day 1;
Thor's-Daeg at sunset began **night** 2; the next sunrise was day 2;
Frigga-Daeg at sunset began night 3; the next sunrise began day 3.
TOTAL: **3 days and 3 nights.**

At sunset as the **weekly** Shabath drew to a close, Yahusha rose from the dead. The **discovery** of His resurrection was not until the following morning when Miryam of Migdal arrived on the first day of the week and found the stone had been removed, and the body was missing. This morning was First-fruits. Yahusha (Kohen haGadol) ascended to the Father as the **wave-sheaf offering.** This is why He would not allow Miryam to **touch** Him; He had not yet presented Himself as the wave-sheaf.
His **resurrected body** was the First-fruits offering, what the barley sheaf had represented.

Yahusha and the 12 were eating a meal at the beginning of the 14th day of the moon, and it was a Tyr's-Daeg evening/night. It was this same night He was arrested, and the following morning He was whipped and put on a stake. That afternoon He died as our Passover Lamb. The confusion is not helped by the fact that the Roman days begin at midnight, instead of the proper time, at sunset. This misunderstanding by Christianity has been the reason that many of us have often said they can't count – but it's really only a stronghold of false teaching, and being removed from the true faith of the Mashiak for so long. They have a "form" of piousness, but deny its authority over them;

they have no Passover, festival of Matsah, Shabouth, Yom Teruah,
Yom Kafar, nor Sukkoth - the "shadows" of redemption-things to come.
By dancing around with their "Sun-day," they miss the foundation because
they did not build on it in the first place.
They modelled their observances after *sun-worshippers*, abandoning all the
festivals of Yisharal, Yahusha's true bride/wife (casuistry, deceptive reasoning).

MEMORIAL OF YAHUSHA'S DEATH

The three days and three nights in the tomb are the "sign of Yunah,"
proving by this sign He is the Mashiak.
The resurrected body of Yahusha is the offering of **First-fruits,** also known as
the **Wave-sheaf offering.** This is why it happened the *"morrow after the
Shabath,"* what Christians call *Sun-day morning*.

The resurrection was rehearsed by the High Priests of Yisharal each time
they cut the **First-fruits** of barley and waved it. Yahusha made it a reality.
He ended the need for ceremonial sin offerings forever.

"In the first month, on the 14th day (ABIB 14) **of the month, between the
evenings, is the Passover to Yahuah. And on the 15th day** (ABIB 15) **of this
month is the Festival of Unleavened Bread to Yahuah – 7 days you eat
unleavened bread.
On the first day you have a set-apart miqra, you do no servile work.
And you shall bring an offering made by fire to Yahuah for seven days.
On the 7th day is a set-apart miqra, you do no servile work.'
And Yahuah spoke to Mosheh, saying, 'Speak to the children of
Yisharal, and you shall say to them, 'When you come into the land which
I give you, and shall reap its harvest, then you shall bring a sheaf of
the first-fruits of your harvest to the priest. And he shall wave the sheaf
before Yahuah for your acceptance.
On the morrow after the Shabath** (weekly) **the priest waves it.
". . . And the morrow after the Shabath, from the day that you brought
the sheaf of the wave offering, you shall count for yourselves:
7 complete** (intact) **Sabbaths.
Until the morrow after the seventh Sabbath you count fifty days, then
you shall bring a new grain offering to Yahuah."** – Lev. / Uyiqra 23:5-16

Teaching that the wave-sheaf offering is always on ABIB 16 is an error,
since on ABIB 16 Yahusha was in the tomb, fulfilling the sign of Yunah.

WE ARE HIS WITNESSES

He healed the sick, raised the dead, walked on water, was dead for three
days and three nights, and rose from the dead. If you read YashaYahu 43,
then read Yahukanon 18, you will see a powerful witness of Who Yahusha is.
At YashaYahu 43, Yahuah tells us we are His witnesses that *He is Alahim*.
He particularly emphasized how we would know this, and be His witnesses to
the gentiles. He said, "*I am He*" in such a way that *it knocked men down*.
First, YashaYahu quotes Him:
**"'You are My witnesses,' declares Yahuah, 'And My servant whom I have
chosen, so that you know and believe Me, and understand that *I am He*.**

Before Me there was no Al formed, nor after Me there is none.
I, *I am Yahuah*, and besides Me there is no deliverer. I, I have declared and delivered, and made known, and there was no foreign mighty one among you. And you are My witnesses,' declares Yahuah 'that I am Al. Even from the day, *I am He*, and no one delivers out of My hand. I work, and who turns it back?" - Is / YashaYahu 43:10-13

Now look at how Yahusha announced "**I am He**" at Yahukanon 18:4-6:
"Yahusha then, knowing all that would come upon Him, went forward and said to them, 'Whom do you seek?
They answered Him, Yahusha of Natsarith.' Yahusha said to them, 'I am He." And Yahudah, who delivered Him up, was also standing with them. When, therefore, He said to them, *'I am He,'* they drew back and fell to the ground."

THE OLDEST LIE OF THEM ALL:
"You Don't Have To Obey"

Yahusha is the *goal* of Torah, not the *end* of Torah. Every Sun-day morning, masses rush into a steeple to listen to a man tell them they don't have to obey, and *they pay him to tell them to disobey!* If they obey, they're heretics.
"For I bear them witness that they have an ardour for Yahuah, but not according to knowledge. For not knowing the uprightness of Yahuah, and seeking to establish their own uprightness, they did not subject themselves to the uprightness of Yahuah. For Mashiak is the goal of the Torah to uprightness to everyone who believes." – Romans 10:2-4 BYNV
The highest pursuit (or purpose) is to learn how to love, and be loved.
The **witness of Yahusha** (or great commission) is to teach the instructions of love to all, but these instructions have been interpreted to be a law that ended with Yahusha's death.
If one reads the instructions as being our best hope in learning how to love, the false idea of being about religion falls away. The universe obviously didn't create itself; its *purpose for being created* tells us so.
The One that created the universe expressed the highest possible thoughts of love, and how to *live that love* - *in His Ten Commandments.*
"And He answering, said to them, 'Well did YashaYahu prophesy concerning you hypocrites, as it has been written, "This people respect Me with their lips, but their heart is far from Me. And in vain do they worship Me, teaching as teachings the commands of men." Forsaking the Command of Alahim, you hold fast the tradition of men.' And He said to them, 'Well do you set aside the command of Alahim, in order to guard your tradition.'" – Mark 7:6-9
With Yahusha's words in mind, what **traditions** have come to replace the Commands of Yahuah?
Christmas; Easter; Sunday; Halloween (feast of dead saints); sacraments; steeples; bells; crosses; eating unclean animals; apostolic succession; celibacy; veneration of human remains and images; holy water; indulgences; Trinitarian ideas; prayer beads; prohibition of the true Name Yahusha; prayers to the dead

(necromancy); infant baptism; *and much more.*

Men have set aside the Commands of Yahuah *for their traditions.*
We find ourselves in exactly the same position of the Pharisees.
Most people are unaware of how much **futility** we have inherited.
In Yahusha's power, our mission is to wake them up.
**"Man shall not live by bread alone, but by every Word that
proceeds from the mouth of Yahuah."** - Mt. 4:4

DAY OF YAHUAH

This is the day Babel's reign ends, and Yahusha's reign begins.

Mat 24:28, 29: **"For wherever the dead body is, there the eagles
shall be gathered together . . . And immediately after the distress
of those days the sun shall be darkened, and the moon shall not
give its light, and the stars shall fall from the heaven, and the
powers of the heavens shall be shaken."** Yual (Joel) 2 and Acts 2 tell us:
"Whoever calls upon the Name of Yahuah will be delivered."
Yahusha seals His property, so the REAPERS will not harm what
belongs to Him. We are sealed for the day of our redemption.

Our Redeemer is on His way, and the fallen malakim know their time
is short. People believing in a pre-Trib rapture will make some
adjustments in their expectations, and come to accept the reality
unfolding around them. Most of them today are Sun-day Sabbath
people, and many are becoming **Natsarim** – (Acts 24:5), end-time
harvest workers. Our most important work during the time of distress
will be to help them be restored to the Covenant of Yahuah, His **Torah,**
the message of AliYahu. (Mal 4:1-6)
WITHOUT WARNING, ONE DAY THE SUN WILL SUDDENLY GO OUT,
AND IN A MOMENT THE ENTIRE SOLAR SYSTEM WILL BE IN DEEP
DARKNESS. THE DAY OF OUR REDEMPTION WILL COME, AND WE
CAN LOOK UP EXPECTANTLY. THE MESSENGERS WILL BE SENT TO
REAP THE HARVEST OF THE EARTH. FIRST, THEY WILL GATHER THE
WEEDS TO BURN THEM. THEN, THOSE FOUND KEEPING THE
COMMANDMENTS OF YAHUAH AND WAITING FOR YAHUSHA WILL BE
GATHERED FOR THE WEDDING FEAST (SUKKOTH, TABERNACLES) AT
THE COMING OF YAHUSHA. DO NOT BE AFRAID. COMFORT ONE
ANOTHER WITH THESE WORDS.
*"But the Day of Yahuah shall come as a thief in the night, in
which the heavens shall pass away with a great noise, and the
elements shall melt with intense heat, and the earth and the
works that are in it shall be burned up."* - 2Pe 3:10
*"And the present heavens and the Earth are treasured up by the
same Word, being kept for fire, to a day of judgment and*

destruction of wicked men." - 2Pe 3:7

"And now, be wise, O sovereigns; be instructed, you rulers of the Earth. Serve Yahuah with fear, and rejoice with trembling. Kiss the Son, lest He be enraged, and you perish in the way, for soon His wrath is to be kindled. Blessed are all those taking refuge in Him." - Psa 2:10-12 (See also Acts 17:30-31)

ALL HUMANITY WILL BE SCREAMING FOR THEIR LIVES

"Remember the Torah of Mosheh, My servant, which I commanded him in Horeb for all Yisharal – laws and right-rulings. See, I am sending you AliYahu the prophet before the coming of the great and awesome day of Yahuah. And he shall turn the hearts of the fathers to the children, and the hearts of the children to their fathers, lest I come and smite the earth with utter destruction." Mal 4:4-6

After the reapers come, we'll be snatched-away just as the Scriptures describe, but it will be at the end of the Distress. (Mat 24:29-31) Yahusha explained how He would send His malakim to the ends of the Earth to gather His elect, so we won't be using transports of any human design. As part of **our** preparation to endure the Distress, Yahusha foretold certain events. He specifically described the darkening of the Sun. Most people reject our words now, but a time is coming when they will beg to listen.

Events will occur that no one will be able to ignore.

Everyone not sealed for protection - *Elitists, homosexuals, secular humanists, abortionists, atheists, agnostics, the media, and those who practice false religion* - will experience a breakdown in their sanity. Reading *Harry Potter* books won't help anyone with what's coming. Minds will snap, and hearts will melt within all mankind.

Because we know His Name, Yahusha wants us, His body, to be aware of coming events in order to spare us the terrible **fear** that others will face. Read Ps 91 as it relates to what you are about to learn.

Kepha/Peter quoted the prophet Yual/Joel in Acts 2 describing the end of days: *"And I shall give signs in the heavens and upon the Earth: blood and fire and columns of smoke; the sun is turned into darkness, and the moon into blood, before the coming of the great and awesome Day of Yahuah. And it shall be that everyone who calls on the Name of Yahuah shall be delivered. For on Mount Tsiyon and in Yerushalayim there shall be an escape as Yahuah has said, and among the survivors whom Yahuah calls."* - Yual 2:30-32; also Act 2:21,2:39; Rom 10:13, Isa 4:2-3, Obad v. 17, Rev. 14:1

Notice there will be an **escape** for those on Mount Tsiyon and in Yerushalayim, *AND* among the *survivors* whom Yahuah *calls*, who will be scattered elsewhere on the Earth. If we take the words **literally** (the sun turned into darkness, and the moon into blood), the study of cosmology helps explain what we will witness. The most frightening thing for everyone alive on this planet will be the sudden darkening of the Sun. We are told in advance about this severe sign *so that we would not be afraid.* Many people will simply drop dead when they experience the fright of the Sun turning dark.

THE NUTS & BOLTS

The sun is in *equilibrium*, balanced between the outward pressure of its thermonuclear process and the inward gravitational pull caused by its mass. The phrase *"moon into blood"* describes an optical principal of the light spectrum. When the sun goes out, it will be Yahuah temporarily stopping the thermonuclear activity deep inside the sun, where hydrogen is constantly being converted into helium (fusion), under extreme pressure and temperature. It's like a constant outward explosion from the core of the sun. When this process stops, the *photosphere* (visible shell of glowing gas) of the Sun will undergo an immediate spectral change toward the red, and the gas ball will utterly go out like a campfire. It will still glow very brightly in the red part of the spectrum from the sheer **heat** stored in the core and outer regions. This is what will make the moon seem to be the color of **blood**, reflecting the light from the reddened sun. The heliosphere, or solar wind, will essentially cease to exist. The Sun will have become a red-dwarf star. Because the outward pressure will temporarily stop, the Sun's mass will cause it to shrink to less than half its current perceived size. As scary as this whole scenario sounds, what follows is even worse. When the sun re-ignites from the pressure of the collapsing gas, there will be a solar nova, or burst of heat, light, and plasma. This will seriously scorch the Earth, and many will be burned to a crisp. The oceans will be moved out of their places, and islands will be annihilated. Coastlands will be lashed clean. All of these things have been described by the prophets of Yahuah, and Yahusha also warned us of them (Mt 24). Kepha (Peter) spoke of it also, at 2 Pet. chapters 2 & 3. This outpouring of **wrath** on the rebellious will not harm those steadfast in the Covenant, for we will be changed, clothed with immortality, just as these events begin to unfold.

"A thousand fall at your side, and ten thousand at your right hand; but it does not come near you." - Ps 91:7

We are guarded by messengers now. It will become obvious in the distress:

"No evil befalls you, and a plague does not come near your tent; for He commands His messengers concerning you, to guard you in all your ways." Ps 91:10,11 (tent = your body). We will be protected from even stubbing our toe on the **Day of Yahuah.**

Extending over the entire Earth, it will be like the *plague of darkness* in the land of Egypt. Added to all this excitement, "stars" (meteors) will fall from the sky, causing some to blaspheme Yahuah. Some of these meteors will be near planet-killers, causing the Earth to reel like a drunkard from the breaking up of the crust, exposing magma. It will literally be the worst period seen since the Earth was created. Those living anywhere within hundreds of miles of a volcano or crustal plate edge will be **consumed by lava**. Yahusha promised to shorten the days for our sakes. Then He will appear in the skies, and every eye will see Him coming. The transgressors and those who resist His Sovereignty will be hiding themselves in the caves, and under rocks, in tunnels they've prepared.

"And the fourth messenger poured out his bowl on the Sun, and it was given to him to burn men with fire. And men were burned with great heat, and they blasphemed the Name of Alahim Who possesses authority over these plagues. And they did not repent, to give Him esteem." - Rev 16:8,9 Clearly the Sun will burn mankind.

"Howl, for the day of Yahuah is near! It comes as a destruction from the Almighty. Therefore all hands go limp, every man's heart melts, and they shall be afraid. Pangs and sorrows take hold of them, they are in pain as a woman in labor; They are amazed at one another, their faces aflame! See, the day of Yahuah is coming, fierce, with wrath and heat of displeasure, to lay the Earth waste, and destroy its sinners from it." - YashaYahu / Isa 13:6-9
False teachings about *when* we will be changed cause many people to believe they will not be on Earth to witness the wrath. Rather, we will be taken (or snatched) by Yahusha as He is returning in the skies, coming to take dominion over this lost world. Our Redeemer comes to take us to Himself, so we must not fear the wrath being poured out. As the lost will feel the terror, we will feel the love of His presence as He comes to gather us on the day of His return.

Look carefully at each component of the following text, describing the Distress, followed by the *gathering* of the qodeshim. Mat 24:29-31:

"And immediately after the distress of those days the sun shall be darkened, and the moon shall not give its light, and the stars shall fall from the heaven, and the powers of the heavens shall be shaken. And then the sign of the Son of Adam shall appear in the heaven, and then all the tribes of the Earth shall mourn, and they shall see the Son of Adam coming on the clouds of the heaven with power and much esteem.

And He shall send His messengers with a great sound of a trumpet, and they shall gather together His chosen ones from the four winds, from one end of the heavens to the other."
If you noticed, these events describe a period of distress (Great Trib), followed by the grand finale, the darkening of the sun.

Next, a meteorite bombardment commences, and the powers of the heavens "shake." *"And then,"* Yahusha appears in the skies, apparently while the sun remains darkened. At this point, a great "shofar" is heard, and the messengers (malakim) are sent to gather the chosen ones. It is at this point the **sealed** Torah-obedient followers of Yahusha are really gathered. It should be obvious to all readers now; the Christian "rapture" ideas are incorrect, and are dangerous because so many will be unproductive harvest workers, paralyzed by the false expectations they were given. Yahusha wants them to return to the Covenant NOW, so they might be added to us to do His work among the lost in the days ahead. *" . . . pray the Master of the harvest to send out workers into His harvest."* - Lk 10:2

The majority of Christians have been listening to poisonous teachings, making them unprepared to stand in the day of wrath. These are the survivors whom Yahuah will call, *assisted by the Natsarim who will be on Earth during the distress.* The Natsarim are the elect (chosen ones) for whom the *duration* of the distress will be shortened.

Our purpose during the distress will be to help people be restored to the Covenant. They must be helped to overcome many false teachings learned from misguided preachers. They will learn that Sun-day is *not the day Yahuah blessed*, and because of their distress, *they will listen to us more closely*. They will not argue about the true Name, and many will submit to immersion for the remission of sin, and be sealed for protection. Those teachers who hold to the "pre-Trib rapture" in spite of the above texts claim that those being gathered in the end of days are those who turned to Yahuah *during* the distress. Christian assemblies believe they will see nothing of the terrors and birth-pangs, and the fiery cataclysm at the very end of days. They believe they are *"in heaven"* during the distress, and will come with Yahusha when He returns. The text says we will all **see** Him coming, be **gathered** by malakim into the *air* to meet Him, and continue down with Him as the New Yerushalayim. This is when the malakim gather the wheat into the Master's barn. We never go to a heaven as most understand "heaven." We will reign with Yahusha in His "Kingdom of heaven," here on a renewed Earth. His Throne will be *on Earth*, and we will be with Him always. Amus 5 and Yual 2 explain to us that the Day of Yahuah is a day of great darkness, and Yahusha's words at Mt. 24 are given to us so we will be comforted when we see the sun literally turn off like a lamp. It will still be glowing RED-HOT, but it will be so dark that we would be struck with terror if we didn't realize what was going on.

"For the Master Yahuah does no matter unless He reveals His secret to His servants the prophets.
A lion has roared! Who is not afraid? The Master Yahuah has spoken! Who would not prophesy? Amus 3:7,8

124

"And there shall be signs in the Sun, and Moon, and stars, and on the Earth anxiety of nations, in bewilderment at the roaring of the sea, and agitation, men fainting from fear and the expectation of what is coming on the Earth, for the powers of the heavens shall be shaken. And then they shall see the Son of Adam coming in a cloud with power and much esteem. And when these matters begin to take place, look up and lift up your heads, because your redemption draws near." - Lk 21:25-28

The Sun and Moon are not symbolic for worldly rulers as some teach today. The darkness will be real, not figurative. This article is written to awaken many from their slumbering, and to prepare us all for what lies *just ahead of us.* Purge the false teachings, *and be sober.*

THE DAY OF YAHUAH IS COMING - 1Th 4:15, 16

"For this we say to you by the Word of the Master, that we, the living who are left over at the coming of the Master shall in no way go before those who are asleep. Because the Master Himself shall come down from heaven with a shout, with the voice of a chief messenger, and with the trumpet of Alahim, and the dead in Mashiak shall rise first. Then we, the living who are left over, shall be caught away together with them in the clouds to meet the Master in the air – and so we shall always be with the Master. So, then, encourage one another with these words."

"'For look, the day shall come, burning like a furnace, and all the proud, and every wrongdoer shall be stubble. And the day that shall come shall burn them up,' said Yahuah Tsabaoth, 'which leaves to them neither root nor branch. But to you who fear My Name, the Servant of Righteousness shall arise with healing in His wings. And you shall go out and leap for joy like calves from the stall. And you shall trample the wrongdoers, for they shall be ashes under the soles of your feet on the day that I do this,' said Yahuah Tsabaoth.

Remember the Torah of Mosheh, My servant, which I commanded him in Horeb for all Yisharal – laws and right-rulings.

See, I am sending you AliYahu the prophet before the coming of the great and awesome Day of Yahuah.

And he shall turn the hearts of the fathers to the children, and the hearts of the children to their fathers, lest I come and smite the Earth with utter destruction.'" - Mal 4:1-6

**LOOK CLOSELY AT THE NYMPHS BELOW, SYMBOLS OF DAGON,
THE FISH DEITY OF THE PHILISTINES:**

It's all witchcraft in plain sight.

**EGYPTIAN: QUEEN OF HEAVEN NUT, AND THE MAZZAROTH
NOTICE ZOO / ZODIAC AT HER SIDES**

NIMROD, ORION, OSIRIS, SERAPIS, BAAL, KRISHNA, RA, GOTT,
ZEUS, MITHRAS, APOLLO, HELIOS, SHAMMASH, ARE THE SAME

MATSAH - UNLEAVENED BREAD
When you learn what it is, you'll see it everywhere.
This funky mold is a cancer, and Yahusha is the cure

A yoke is a body of teachings. From What Yoke Does The Truth Set Us Free? Most people have the impression it concerns **the Ten Commandments, and Yahuah's festivals**. This is tragic because this is the strong delusion. The Ten Commandments are in fact the **Truth**, and a **Light** for our path. The Truth frees us from a smelly fungus, and there's even a special 7-day observance Yahuah commanded for us to observe every year to *clean it out*.

Our freedom is from the traditions of men, which Yahusha was the most critical of above all else. Yahusha calls the teachings of men **"leaven."** He was never upset because anyone obeyed the Ten Commandments, but rather because they disobeyed them and made men's traditions their commandments.

The seven-day observance called Unleavened Bread (Matsah) is a shadow of redemption that pictures the removal of the **moldy, puffed-up teaching authority of men from our hearts**, so **our hearts** are able to receive the pure, clean teachings of Yahusha, free of the corrupting ideas of men.

Yahusha was upset with how traditions came to replace the Commandments of Yahuah. If Yahusha were to appear in person at a Sunday morning assembly,

He would surely see nothing that reflects how He taught us to live, because Constantine insisted that they would have **"nothing in common with the hostile rabble of the Yahudim."** Most still have Constantine's mold in their hearts. This is a small glimpse at the **festival of Matsah**, one of **seven observances** of Yahuah.

They are the redemption plan, a shadow of things to come.

"Do not make idols for yourselves and do not set up a carved image or a pillar for yourselves, and do not place a stone image in your land, to bow down to it. For I am Yahuah your Alahim."

ONLY YAHUSHA CAN RESTORE EYESIGHT TO THE BLIND
RECEIVE YAHUSHA'S TORAHVISION
HE IS OUR ONLY TEACHING AUTHORITY

WHAT IS A CHURCH?
A Sun Temple?
Lev. 26
DO NOT MAKE PILLARS
TORAH INSTITUTE

"There is a way that seems right to a man,
But its end is the way of death." - Proverbs 16:25

NIMROD STARTED ALL THIS
and Yahusha will end it.
He will burn it down at His coming.

For more books by this author:
www.torahzone.net